"Danielle Hensley takes us i[...] between a person and their s[...] timate, and deeply moving ex[...] are shared. The reader has an extraordinary vantage point: one is looking right into the heart of a family divided by faith and politics. A remarkable journey; this is a book that is sure to become a classic of its kind."

—Ian S. Markham, dean and president, Virginia Theological Seminary

"Danielle Hensley does what so many of us want to do but don't: she tells hard truths, but manages to do so from a place of unconditional love. Speaking truth to power is not for the faint of heart. The stories and hard-won lessons she shares in this book will help readers to summon the courage to be brave in the face of injustice—even when the face is familiar (or familial). May we all be as brave and kind as she."

—Cathleen Falsani, author of *Sin Boldly: A Field Guide for Grace*

"With keen insight, limpid prose, and infinite patience, Danielle Hensley probes the challenge many of us are facing these days: How to deal with avowedly Christian family and loved ones who have succumbed to the cult of Donald Trump."

—Randall Balmer, author of *Bad Faith: Race and the Rise of the Religious Right*

"A candid memoir of one woman's political awakening and the local and personal consequences amid the tensions that have created national divisions. This is the story of the seeming impossibility of compromise on either side—and the resulting, tragic 'divorce' of a family."

—Jill Peláez Baumgaertner, author of *From Shade to Shine: Selected Poems*

If the Bough Breaks . . .

If the Bough Breaks . . .

When Faith and Politics Bend a Family Tree
to Its Breaking Point

Danielle Hensley

CASCADE *Books* · Eugene, Oregon

IF THE BOUGH BREAKS . . .
When Faith and Politics Bend a Family Tree to Its Breaking Point

Cascade Books
An Imprint of Wipf and Stock Publishers
199 W. 8th Ave., Suite 3
Eugene, OR 97401

www.wipfandstock.com

PAPERBACK ISBN: 978-1-6667-8985-0
HARDCOVER ISBN: 978-1-6667-8986-7
EBOOK ISBN: 978-1-6667-8987-4

Cataloguing-in-Publication data:

Names: Hensley, Danielle [author].
Title: If the bough breaks . . . : when faith and politics bend a family tree to its breaking point / by Danielle Hensley.
Description: Eugene, OR: Cascade Books, 2024 | Includes bibliographical references.
Identifiers: ISBN 978-1-6667-8985-0 (paperback) | ISBN 978-1-6667-8986-7 (hardcover) | ISBN 978-1-6667-8987-4 (ebook)
Subjects: LCSH: Trump, Donald, 1946– —Religion. | Christianity and politics—United States. | Religious Right—United States. | Presidents—United States—Election—2016. | Presidents—United States—Election—2020. | Presidents—United States—Election—2024. | Autobiographies.
Classification: BR526 H46 2024 (paperback) | BR526 (ebook)

VERSION NUMBER 04/26/24

"All Sheep Matter" cartoon by David Hayward aka NakedPastor. Used by permission.

For Mom and Dad:

There is so much love here.
I hope you see it, too.

If I love you, I have to make you conscious of the things you don't see.

—James Baldwin

Content

Illustrations:

Dearest Danielle

Sent: Monday, January 11, 2021, 3:47 PM
To: dhensley
Subject: Re: I'm sorry.

Dearest Danielle,

Usually, I would write a personal letter in response to something as important as our mother-daughter relationship. Thank you for writing. Before going any further—yes, you are forgiven and there is nothing that would ever stop me from loving you completely. Our bond made in utero cannot be dissolved in my heart or mind.

Danielle, you have always been your own person, since toddler stage, and now you are growing into another chapter at fifty when what you think and believe is mentored to your own children who can speak with their own thoughts and feelings. And, they are wonderful kids, our grand kids. You have spunk and passion. You said you want to tame her [i.e., your feisty nature]. It is hard to harness the wind. I love that phrase, not sure where it comes from, though. Fresh winds blow in new possibilities, and wind can destroy. So, we'll go forward on new wind for new possibilities.

This last year has been so trying and has brought lots of things to a head that were brewing politically for many years. Presently, I need to take a step into solitude, not to escape but to let my mind (that is not always as quick as others) and soul/faith give direction. Raw and sad are the two words that describe us now.

When anyone talks to me about the state of affairs (they talk—I listen), my question at the end is: What can each of us do to make a difference in the right direction? You have gifts that give me reason to believe you can be in the public square someplace encouraging, mentoring, leading. God will show you because you desire to be shown. For me, I will continue to be a listener and point folks to try to understand where people are. But most of all, where might we witness to truth and serve as lovers of truth?

I don't give people answers; I pray with them. When I must speak or preach, I want to represent what good the Lord has in store for each person, and our country as one people. So, I will continue to pray for you, our family, myself, and let the Lord direct us as we encourage each other. God is able to do exceedingly well that which we cannot.

Many hugs dear Danielle. I love you so very much, am blessed to have you for a daughter, and now as a grown up to offer this mother things to think about, challenges to climb, and love to scatter for others.

Mom

Acknowledgments

I give a heartfelt thanks to my co-worker, Molly Edmonds, who was the first to lay eyes on a very fragmented manuscript (even before my husband and children knew of its existence), and saw the potential and told me to keep pulling the thread. So I did. Then came Dr. Stacia Pelletier, who wanted to know about *me*—how do *I* fare as a character in this story? "The reader will want to know," she said. So I reflected. With a more complete book-in-the-making, my college friend Dr. Stephen Woodburn graciously provided copious comments, corrections about historical facts, and helpful insights about my writing. If you want an honest and thoughtful response, Steve is your guy, and I am forever grateful he said "yes." By the time Cathleen Falsani (another fellow Wheatie) from Sinners and Saints Creative came on board, I was contemplating publication. With Cathleen's guidance, and her uncanny ability to find the wound and gently massage it, the final stages of writing, while all about the book, also became nothing about the book. I was crawling through the weeds, but Cathleen could see the bigger picture, knowing full well the implications of this book. So I pursued. I'd also like to thank family, friends, and acquaintances along the way who encouraged me at various points of the project: Linnea Lowe, Helen Moses, Courtney Carroll, Dr. Sue Schrock, Dr. Chris Matson, and Dr. Randall Balmer. I'm also grateful to the Rev. Jamie Pahl for introducing me to the dean and president of Virginia Theological Seminary, the Very Rev. Ian S. Markham, PhD, who put me in touch with my editor, the Rev. Dr. Robin Parry at Cascade Books. And finally, to my husband and children—especially my brave daughter, who gave me permission to tell her story—to all three of them who buoyed me through some tumultuous storms to arrive at safer shores: thank you.

INTRODUCTION _____

Trumpocalypse Now

> I sat with my anger long enough until she told me
> her real name was grief.
>
> —C. S. Lewis

I n February 2021, I emailed my sister with a proposition:

> On my walk this morning, I got to thinking a bit more about
> doing a joint project. A book? Possibly. But what might be more
> interesting is a blog because it shows a work in progress, which
> is what we are attempting. We could take turns posting a ques-
> tion/problem/observation, and we each respond to it indepen-
> dently—posting our responses side-by-side. We can then come
> back and find elements of commonality, points of difference, and
> then next steps or something like that.
>
> I think the two of us have a unique relationship in that we
> have so many social indicators that are similar (same parents, same
> school, active in our churches, love family, protect relationships,
> etc.), and yet we differ so much on politics and even religion. Still,
> perhaps we might find more similarities than we realize.
>
> Perhaps this could be a really interesting endeavor that not
> only will help us but others as well who are trying to navigate
> the current divide in America. It might not go anywhere, but
> I'm sure it will help. And then if we become rich and famous, or
> at the very least, a blogging sensation, then we can have famous
> people like Brené Brown comment. JK.
>
> Same Tree, Different Branch
>
> Thoughts?
>
> D.

I did not set out to write a book, and had I ever imagined writing one, this certainly would not have been it. Not by a long shot. I wrote out of sheer compulsion because I could not, for the life of me, understand my family's draw to a personality like Trump. Perhaps you've felt this confusion, too? While my story is unique, it's also universal because it's about the fierce love of family and the desperate desire to keep it together. I'm hoping you'll come along with me: learn from my mistakes, take the parts that resonate with you, think about how you might be the change in your own family and friendship circles, and then do the hard work. Change starts with you and me.

But before two people can collaborate, they must agree on some *thing*, right? While my sister's initial enthusiasm about my blog suggestion was affirming, I eventually discovered that in her attempt to please, she has a difficult time saying no. Even after I followed up with her about the joint project several times, she would neither commit to it nor outright decline it, so I eventually just stopped asking.

Perhaps her hesitancy came from the fact that we can't even agree on the meaning of individual words let alone use them collectively in a sentence. Or perhaps the emotional grafting work would prove too difficult on a relationship with roots already exposed.

Families are complicated. If you are invested in one, you understand the push-pull of obligations and expectations, the persistent urge to chart one's own path while, somehow, remaining in the fold. At least that's been my experience. Now, add religion and politics to the mix.

The 2016 presidential election led me into uncharted territory, a crossroads of politics and religion where I held a map without a key. Since friends, neighbors, and even clergy, many of them just as bewildered as I was, were unable to provide the directions I needed, I went looking for answers myself by heading straight to the source.

When millions of Americans voted for a thrice-married reality TV personality and notorious New York social climber/grifter with zero political experience, I wrote off the 2016 election as a colossal political science experiment gone bad. But when roughly half of Americans once again aligned with Trump in the 2020 election cycle, I needed help understanding how anyone could support him after all that we've seen and heard. More specifically, I desperately needed an explanation about how my amazingly loving, highly educated, and deeply faith-filled family[1] could

---

1. I define "family" in this book as my nuclear family of origin consisting of my sister, mother, and father. I have redacted their names to provide privacy.

support a president who is antithetical to everything we profess to believe and are supposed to embody as Christians.

As is the nature of most quests, what I sought was the thing *not* found.

I love my family. And if you know them, I know you do too because they are just plain affable. They exude kindness and hospitality. And their ability to draw you out and find commonalities is their collective super-power, a fact proven when my dad is consistently the last person out of church each Sunday. If you are new to the neighborhood, expect a knock on the door followed by an official welcome and some homemade cookies. If you rang our doorbell during the dinner hour, my mother would insist you come inside, and before you could refuse, she'd already have a place setting ready for you at the table. If you were hospitalized, they'd come visit. My sister and I saw this type of love and support every day. My parents humored every sport I tried—from softball to volleyball to swimming—often cheering embarrassingly loud, so much that I begged them to stop. I gleaned my love of science fiction from my dad, who was the first in line to watch *Star Wars*. My appreciation for Tolkien and L'Engle followed next. Of course, going out for ice cream always meant two scoops. And don't even get me started about amusement parks and rides. I led a charmed life, but mostly I was supported and very loved. And that's a big reason why I never cared about which political party they supported—in the day-to-day, it just didn't matter.

My family has always been Republican. Not the type to wear MAGA hats and wave Trump flags at political rallies. Quite the contrary. My family members carry their Republican cards quietly, supporting fiscal conservatism, small government, and gun rights; they are anti-abortion, pro-military, and defend religious rights without bumper stickers, yard signs, or other fanfare. In voting for Trump, they were just doing what they normally did. Business as usual. How could I fault them for that? In fact, as a young adult, I'd even been known to bat for their team on several occasions. Because I respect *them*, I'd never questioned my family's voting history because voting for their choice of candidate is their right, and as American as apple pie.

At least I thought it was until Trump came along. When my family stayed the course, many of them supporting Trump's new Republican Party even after four years of his chaotic, depraved, and dishonest administration, I had a political epiphany and fell headfirst into a huge existential crisis.

Politics, which presented my steepest learning curve, was the source of only half my angst. The other half is my Christian identity. My parents raised us in the Episcopal Church. As an adult, I stayed, but my sister migrated to the nondenominational/evangelical church. Still, we are, all of us, Christians: we profess Jesus' death on the cross and his resurrection, we attend church regularly, we tithe, we participate in various forms of church ministry, we give of our time and talents, and we pray. Most importantly, we attempt to be the hands and feet of Christ in the world because we are called to love our neighbors as ourselves. However, each of us interprets and acts upon that gospel mandate differently, and as the Trump years wore on, those differences became increasingly untenable.

My political awakening was not instantaneous, like flipping a switch. It was more of a groggy emergence from a long, deep sleep. Like any journey of self-discovery—religious, political, racial, and otherwise—there is an impulse to make up for lost time. We rewind and replay the past, connecting fragments of memory and history to try to make sense of the present. It's part of our nature to fill in the gaps with our personal narrative when things don't make sense within the context of our family systems. And the story we tell (and tell ourselves) often gets passed on to the next generation with neither discussion nor critical lens. The narrative that has played in my head for the last fifty-plus years is precisely what I am now trying to understand. The excavation has been arduous but necessary work that promotes growth. Then comes the pruning.

A real consequence of my awakening has been the strain it has placed on relationships with people I love most. I don't blame my sister for not following through with my blog idea. We both had and have our individual journeys to make before we can come together for productive conversations around religion and politics. I hope we will get there some day. Until then, my solo work here grows from the divide that remains, a fissure between sisters (and other family members) in a family tree that shares the same roots but has branches that have grown in very different directions.

1

The Meme That Opened Pandora's Box

> The god Prometheus stole fire from heaven to give to the human race, which originally consisted only of men. To punish humanity, the other gods created the first woman, the beautiful Pandora. As a gift, Zeus gave her a box, which she was told never to open. However, as soon as he was out of sight, she took off the lid, and out swarmed all the troubles of the world, never to be recaptured. Only Hope was left in the box, stuck under the lid.
>
> —*Merriam-Webster* (online), s.v. "Pandora's Box"

I was not yet born during the "Where were you?" phenomenon that followed President John F. Kennedy's assassination in 1963. But I can tell you exactly where I was and what I was doing when I heard the windows rattle after American Airlines Flight 77 hit the south side of the Pentagon on September 11, 2001. We recently had relocated to the Virginia Theological Seminary in Alexandria, Virginia, for my husband's new job. Living in the Bishop's Suite, our temporary apartment until renovations were completed in our campus house, we caught our breath before the moving van arrived. Our son, just ten months old at the time, was napping in his Pack 'n' Play when my husband called and told me to turn on the television.

I had attributed the windows rattling to nearby construction; however, roughly four miles from where we watched the horror unfold on TV, smoke from jet fuel and burning bodies filled the otherwise cloudless skies on a beautiful autumn morning.

Catastrophic moments become indelibly seared in our individual and collective memories because no one imagined them possible until they happened. The trauma remains long after the shock of the catastrophe itself. It is for that reason that I remember precisely where I was when I learned Donald J. Trump had won the 2016 presidential election. I stayed up as late as I could that election night, but with results slowly trickling in, and the numbers not moving in Hillary Clinton's favor, I decided to go to bed. The kids still had school in the morning and making breakfast and packing lunches would go on as usual, regardless of the outcome. After a few hours of sleep, I woke up, grabbed my phone, and fumbled my way into the bathroom. It was there, while sitting on the toilet, that I decided to check the results. The humor of this visual metaphor is not lost on me now, but at the time, I was grateful for the support the toilet provided should my knees have buckled. For a fleeting second, I willingly remained in ignorance, but my finger impulsively tapped the screen to show me Trump's face grinning from ear to ear.

It feels a bit hyperbolic and perhaps even sacrilegious to compare Trump's presidential win to the horrors of 9/11. Never have we seen anything so horrific and felt so helpless as a country as when the Twin Towers—symbolic pillars of America's strength and its people's success—fell to dust before our eyes. The thing about the aftermath, however, is that 9/11 brought our country together, at least for a time. We did not fold or succumb. Instead, neighbor uplifted neighbor. We bottlenecked the phone systems calling to check on friends and family across the country and around the globe. We mourned as a nation. President George W. Bush offered words of unity and consolation to a traumatized nation: "Today, our nation saw evil, the very worst of human nature. And we responded with the best of America—with the daring of our rescue workers, with the caring for strangers."[1] They were words of hope for a grieving people. For that moment, at least, we felt as if we truly were a United States of America.

Unless, of course, you happened to be a Muslim.

The U.S. government needed to understand the source of such vile acts of terrorism against our democracy that claimed thousands of innocent lives and shook our collective sense of security to its core. Rightly so. Yet finding the identity and backstory of the men who commandeered

---

1. Bush, "Statement by the President," lines 15–16.

all three airplanes gave some Americans license to shun, rebuke, and even threaten our Muslim American neighbors. We had done the same thing, with even more gusto, to our Japanese American neighbors after the bombing of Pearl Harbor in 1941.

It's hardly surprising, then, that more than twenty years after 9/11, our country is more outspokenly and wildly divided than ever. No, Trump didn't create the division; he just fertilized the seed that had already been planted. The source of our national insecurity today is not foreign enemies, such as we saw on 9/11. It has become painfully clear since the "Unite the Right" White supremacist rally in Charlottesville, Virginia, in 2017 and the January 6, 2020, insurrectionist attack on the U.S. Capitol, that our nation is increasingly jeopardized by a breed of emboldened racist and White supremacist domestic terrorists who derive strength and justification from Trump's dehumanizing rhetoric and his lies about a "stolen" election.

Since Trump's term in office, hate crimes increased by 30 percent,[2] and the number of organized White supremacist groups increased by a staggering 55 percent during the Trump administration.[3] When the president told the Proud Boys to "stand back and stand by" during a live, televised debate, I expected Americans to shudder in revulsion. Instead, nearly half of all American voters—including members of my family of origin—were willing to vote for Trump a second time in 2020. And many members seem willing to vote for him yet again in 2024.

Days after the 2016 election, I earnestly tried to give Trump a chance. I really did. I even tried praying for him, but confessed to Beth, my friend and fellow parishioner, that I was completely unable to do so. When our rector, during the Prayers of the People, invited us to pray for our president, world leaders, and all those in authority, I told her I could barely utter the congregational response of *Lord, have mercy*. As Beth's eyes welled up with tears, she nodded in agreement, then leaned in while gently touching my arm and whispered, "It's okay to let others carry the heavy lifting sometimes." But I felt conflicted. Hillary Clinton graciously conceded, so it was my duty as a good citizen to move forward and get behind the new president. That's what Americans do. Even though there were early rumors of Russian interference in our election, it would be years before they could be proven or dispelled. Besides, I rationalized that a smart president with no government or political experience surely would surround himself

---

2. Farivar, "US Hate Crimes Rise," lines 9–11.
3. Wilson, "White Nationalist Hate Groups," lines 1–2.

with qualified people who, at the very least, understand the Constitution and know how our government and laws work.

My suspension of disbelief and chance-giving lasted only a hot minute until Trump failed the litmus test by filling high-level policy-making cabinet and other administrative positions with business tycoons, big donors, and even a former event planner with no experience in government. For me, appointing his daughter and son-in-law, Ivanka and Jared Kushner, as senior White House advisers with top security clearances was the final straw. Many of Trump's supporters voted for him because they believed he was different from the Washington status quo, an outsider who vowed to shake things up. If nothing else, he did, most certainly, succeed at that.

Two weeks after the 2016 presidential election, my father called my sister and me, informing us there would be absolutely no political discussions any time during our impending Thanksgiving celebration that year. Period. The same message trickled down to all the grandchildren. I was worried about this holiday, so his edict came as a relief. Nevertheless, no amount of fair warning could eliminate the underlying tension that upheld our holiday table. Our family tradition of verbalizing a blessing, just as you might pass the mashed potatoes around the table, felt forced and inauthentic. How was I supposed to summon something good when, to me, the election had tilted the earth off its axis? Months later, my mother told me that my father made this declaration to "protect" *me.*

But holidays have a short shelf life. A few months later, while sitting in an oversized leather chair in my sister's living room with both legs hanging over the arm, something happened that heralded an approaching storm. My brother-in-law pulled up a straight-backed wooden chair directly in front of me, turned it backward and straddled the seat while crossing his arms over the back of the chair. Looking me straight in the eye, he asked, "Why, all of a sudden, are you so interested in politics?"

I hate politics. It is best served with a heaping dose of history, and for me, history was my least favorite subject. I respect history, and marvel over those who make a career out of it, but to understand it is like trying to collect water in a sieve. No matter how long you plumb history's depths, there are layers of perspective, opinion, and relics that, once unearthed, could change your trajectory and derail your whole previous understanding. Take, for instance, the false narrative of Christopher Columbus "discovering" America, which supposedly culminated with pilgrims and Indians happily breaking bread together at that first Thanksgiving. Or learning that the GI Bill didn't apply equally to the millions of Black and Brown World War II veterans. Or the dozens of massacres in Black communities that occurred on American soil throughout our history which were conspicuously absent from generations of school curricula. Or most recently, that Rosa Parks refused to sit in the back of the bus *not because she was tired* but because of a well-planned, nonviolent civil rights protest. At the end of the day, politics—history's close cousin—requires you pick a side, take a stand, and if need be, defend your position.

Growing up, my parents' devotion to generosity and hospitality meant we had a revolving door of guests regularly gracing our dinner table—a direct result of our life as a military family. Since every three or four years meant a new assignment for my father, a U.S. Army officer with a doctorate in entomology, and therefore a new location for our family, we learned to adapt to new surroundings quickly. When I was six months old, we moved to Thailand, followed by a tour of duty in Maryland, then Texas, then the Panama Canal Zone, and then back to Maryland—all before I graduated high school. What better way to assimilate to a new place than to invite the neighbors over for a meal?

As a woefully shy child, when the home phone rang, I would become suddenly engrossed in any activity that might prevent me from having to answer it. Even more terrifying was the prospect of having to meet a stranger in person. When being introduced to someone new, I tried to unzip my parents and climb inside their skin to hide. The next best solution involved ducking behind my dad, wrapping both arms around one of his legs and squeezing it like a tourniquet. Because of this shyness, I still am more content to remain on the outside looking in, and I still find my happy place in the background where no one knows I'm listening. So, when dinner conversations moved toward politics, current events, or religion, I would absent myself from the table to quietly refill water glasses or remove dirty dishes. My mother often begged me to come back and join the conversation, but I used the act of servitude to physically remove myself because serving was more comfortable than participating.

At the time, I wouldn't have been able to articulate it, but now I know a thing or two about avoidance. For me, the act of service was just that. It is always well received, but it also acts as a perfect cover because serving requires very little of me except my time and a bit of physical energy. I'm serving you, so I'm the one in control. It's like punching the clock. But actively participating in something, getting dirty and rolling around in it, is a whole other animal. It takes up head space and requires emotional capital. Participating also has the potential to expose my weaknesses and reveal my shortcomings. Serving means spinning my wheels and looking helpful and productive; participating means getting face to face and relational. For this shy kid, serving was the bull's eye in my comfort zone.

My sister mentioned several times how, since the 2016 election, she longs for her "old sister," but how do you stuff the genie back in the bottle? Because I knew this "why now?" question would come eventually, I had rehearsed it in my head multiple times. I, too, had to discover why I was all in—what was different in 2016 that wasn't present in previous election cycles? What specifically had changed in me? Straightening my posture, I told my brother-in-law, as silly as it may sound, my awakening stemmed from a post I saw on social media:

> I want my friends to understand that "staying out of politics" or being "sick of politics" is privilege in action. Your privilege allows you to live a non-political existence. Your wealth, your race, your abilities or your gender allows you to live a life in which you likely will not be a target of bigotry, attacks, deportation, or genocide. You don't want to get political; you don't want to fight because your life and safety are not at stake.
>
> It's hard and exhausting to bring up issues of oppression (aka "get political"). The fighting is tiring, I get it. Self-care is essential. But if you find politics annoying and you just want everyone to be nice, please know that people are literally fighting for their lives and safety. You might not see it, but that's what privilege does.[4]

Without a doubt, my extended family has been completely blindsided by what appears to them to be my new and sudden political awakening. My sister admonished me about my news consumption and told me instead to do something productive in my community. She was right. A few weeks later, I attended the interest meeting for a newly forming refugee outreach program at the Episcopal church we attend, St. Michael's in Raleigh, North Carolina. After hearing the presentation, I knew this work could serve many purposes. Not only would it primarily help fully-vetted people flee religious persecution and human atrocities around the globe, it also would assuage my need to respond with intentionality and purpose to Trump's poorly planned and rashly executed 2017 "Muslim ban."

---

4. @MotherWise, "To my friends who are sick," August 15, 2017.

We watched in horror in January 2017 when Trump signed an executive order banning foreign nationals from seven predominantly Muslim countries from visiting the United States for ninety days, throwing our major international airports into chaos and striking fear into the hearts of countless travelers. News media vans and throngs of protestors jammed the roadways outside arrival and departure halls while immigration lawyers offered free legal counsel, and Muslim American family members anxiously awaited the arrival of their loved ones who had been in mid-flight when Trump's executive order took immediate effect.

My father chose this time to forward the whole family an email, time-stamped August 2017, with the subject line "The Muslim infiltration." The main crux of the message was an unidentified person's paraphrase of Dr. Peter Hammond's book *Slavery, Terrorism and Islam: The Historical Roots and Contemporary Threat*. The body of the email was written in a large blue font and chock-full of numbers and percentages lending an air of credibility. Although my father provided no commentary or context, all I had to do was read other recipients' embedded comments—"This is important to pray about and take action!"—to see that it was my father's not-so-subtle way of giving credence to Trump's xenophobic, racist, and unconstitutional attack on Muslims and Muslim Americans by amplifying an outdated book from a nonacademic conservative Christian self-publishing company.

While the refugee work was rewarding, it only fueled my passion to understand what had drawn my family members to Trump. Interestingly, the more invested I became in the refugee program, the more attention I paid to politics. During my tenure in the group, Trump nearly obliterated the U.S. Refugee Program, a long-standing source of American pride and global citizenship supported by every sitting president until Trump. Redefining a wealthy nation's moral obligation to help oppressed peoples around the globe, Trump stoked nationalism by closing our borders to keep out refugees from "shithole countries."[5] Subsequently, the Trump administration nearly obliterated refugee admittances by systematically reducing the admissions ceiling from its height of 110,000 refugees per year during the Obama administration, to 50,000 refugees in 2017, and then finally to a paltry ceiling of 15,000 before leaving office.[6] As a result of Trump's policy, "for the first time in modern history, the United States settled fewer refugees than the rest of the world, . . . the fewest in any year since the creation

5. Epatko, "How the World," line 1.
6. American Immigration Council, "Overview," September 20, 2021, lines 112, 120.

of the program."[7] As the richest nation in the world, Trump's actions were both morally appalling and patently un-American.

When I was in high school, my parents had volunteered in a refugee resettlement program. In the late 1980s, we supported a family of four seeking asylum from Communist Party rule in the Czech Republic. We set up the Czech family's apartment with extra furnishings from our home, helped the parents find jobs, and registered their children for school. We helped them with language acquisition and to learn the American banking system. The years-long endeavor was slow and often frustrating, but my parents' commitment to showing gratitude for our freedoms by extending hospitality and hands-on assistance to a family who had experienced so few liberties in their homeland was a formative lesson I have never forgotten. Yet Trump's desire to rid America of the same refugee program that had opened our doors to the Czech family thirty years earlier, the program that my parents valued as contributing to the American fabric of diversity and opportunity, did not appear in 2017 or in 2020 to trouble them in the slightest.

How was that possible?

---

7. American Immigration Council, "Overview," September 20, 2021, lines 10–11.

2

Pressure Cookers

The one who plants trees, knowing that he or she will never sit in their shade, has at least started to understand the meaning of life.

—Rabindranath Tagore

Every summer as a kid we would visit grandparents—my dad's parents, the Rev. Rowland N. and Kathryn Alexander, who summered at Dimock Campground, a historic campground in Dimock, Pennsylvania, chartered in 1877 and designated as a United Methodist Church national heritage landmark. It still exists today. Rustic two-story cabins built in a circular fashion around a central green that, in my generation, housed an enormous bonfire pit, a metal swing set, and a porch swing hanging from an ancient tree and wide enough to comfortably seat three adults.

The campground had electricity and running water, but only two landlines—one in the dining hall and the other in my grandparents' living room. The highlights of the summer visits for me were the pond and dock, the white clapboard chapel, and a ping pong table in the dining hall at the top of the hill that long ago was torn down. We roamed the campground like free-range chickens, only coming inside for lunch and dinner. Kick-the-can and fireside s'mores filled our evenings' entertainment to where some nights I'd be too tired for a bath.

The chapel had all the accoutrements of a holy space, including a rustic wooden cross, lectern for a pulpit, and wooden folding stadium seats instead of traditional pews. On Sundays the chapel was holy ground, but every other day of the week it was grounds for hide and seek. My grandfather, an ordained American Baptist minister, preached from the pulpit Sunday mornings during the summer, but the real show stopper was the evening program. As part of Dimock's vision to develop "a variety of programs and activities that will expand opportunities with the community at large,"[1] the schedule included itinerant preachers from various denominations, choral groups, musicians, and other religious entertainers. People from neighboring rural communities from near and far filled just about every seat in God's humble house.

Not only was this program good, old-fashioned hospitality, it also fulfilled Dimock's mission to "invite others to grow in faith."[2] The fastest way to any sinner's heart is with food, and as such, we took Jesus' commandment to "feed my sheep" seriously. All guests were invited to walk up the gravel hill and commune cafeteria-style over rows and rows of desserts of all shapes, sizes, fillings, and frostings. It was the feeding of the multitudes, but instead of five loaves and two fish, a cherry cobbler would miraculously appear to replace the last slice of a lemon pound cake.

Memories of my grandmother involve three things: she was either knitting, sewing, or cooking. For me, she smocked cotton dresses which I saved for my own daughter. And knitting needles, like extensions of her fingers, meant she could count purl stitches while watching TV or having a conversation without ever diverting her eyes. My grandmother gifted every newly married grandchild with one of her prized afghan blankets, and welcomed great grandchildren with a sweater, matching booties, and a baby blanket. No yarn was wasted, either, because hats and scarves started out blue but ended up yellow with a bit of brown in between. From her wake just inside the entrance of the Dimock chapel, my grandmother took a pair of those very knitting needles to her final resting place next to my grandfather in the graveyard behind what is now the Dimock Christian Community Church.

Summer weekends meant several trays of homemade cinnamon buns made from June Benoit's handed-down recipe—some with nuts and some without—but much to my chagrin, all with raisins. Like searching for a fly in the ointment, I'd unroll the gooey buns and systematically pull out and set aside each loathsome squishy, brown fruit. And let me be clear, our family's understanding of "cinnamon bun" did not include the gloppy white frosting made from powdered sugar. No, Grandmother's buns floated on a

1. Dimock Camp Meeting Ground home page, lines 2–3.
2. Dimock Camp Meeting Ground home page, line 1.

pool of Mr. Ely's local honey swirled with half a jar of dark Karo® corn syrup, baked until golden brown, then inverted so the syrup cascaded down onto the plate. Sunday dinner meant baked ham and all the sides. However, the wheezing sound of the pressure cooker, akin to an old-fashioned rotary sprinkler, was her one culinary sin. In addition to that week's vat of soup from the culminated contents of the large pickle jar in the corner of the fridge, she pressure-cooked the life out of broccoli until completely unrecognizable in shape, color, and texture.

While Dad worked on his dissertation in Houston in the mid-70s, my grandparents came for a visit. When they arrived with their car weighted down like the Clampetts from *The Beverly Hillbillies*—minus the rocking chair, of course, but instead filled from roof to trunk with suitcases, a sewing machine, and numerous tubs of my grandmother's various crafts—we welcomed them as we always did. Unbeknownst to my parents, however, instead of staying a week or two, after their arrival my grandfather coyly asked if they could stay for six months.

There was no asking in advance, probably because they knew my dad couldn't refuse once they were already there. My grandfather sheepishly explained to my dad that upon his retirement from full-time ministry, they decided to winterize the Dimock cabin. With little savings and no home to return to, Dimock was their answer to prayer—the same cabin that lacked any form of insulation and featured a kitchen floor that slanted from one side of the house to the other. Not to mention the bats that lived between the rafters in the second-story bunkroom. After rounds of meetings and seeking permission from the Dimock board, they finally got the votes that allowed them to be the first family to retrofit a cabin for year-round living. With a foundation to secure, and structures to reinforce, the task would take months to complete. Where would they stay in the meantime? In my bedroom, they decided.

During these same elementary school years in Texas, I was a latch-key kid. This arrangement was not my parents' first choice by any means, but with my dad working odd hours at the university running labs and gathering data for his dissertation, and my mother working as a nurse at a gynecology clinic for at-risk women, my only other option was day care. But I wasn't having any of that. My sister, already in middle school, would be home an hour or so after my arrival, so I fought tooth and nail to avoid after school care, begging my parents to let me walk home instead. After touring several day care facilities and witnessing my disapproval and overall unhappiness, my parents acquiesced—I was instructed to call my mom at work immediately upon unlocking the front door. If I lingered one second longer than the brisk twenty-minute one-mile walk home, I surely got an earful from my panicked mother who wondered why I took so long getting home.

With my grandparents in town, this latchkey problem resolved itself, but then other problems unleashed. For example, I now came home from school each day to my grandmother usually knitting on the couch. It wasn't long before she started giving me "oughts" and "shoulds," and other unsolicited comments about behavior and attitudes. I wasn't about to have any of that either, and after a day or two, I reminded her that she wasn't my mother. I was not about to be bossed around about chores and homework by an old lady who had taken over my bedroom. After getting nowhere with me directly, my grandmother went to my mother, expecting for her to put a kink in my tail. Instead, my mother told my grandmother to figure it; the two of us needed to come to some sort of agreement. We eventually got there, and the final result gave me a sense of power and some semblance of control. In the end, we made a truce, and my grandmother helped me learn my multiplication tables and how to pronounce difficult words for an upcoming oral book report.

For my birthday during the winter they stayed with us, my grandmother surprised me with a homemade Barbie Doll Bundt cake, the one with the doll balanced in the hole and the cake piped with frosting to resemble her skirt. But the best gift was the Barbie clothing collection she made for me, complete with a lace wedding dress she sewed from remnants. Sadly, her generous gifts of time and talent were too often tempered by the force of her tongue. If gossiping were a spiritual gift, she would surely achieve sainthood. She wasn't the type of grandmother who doted on you, or held you close, or stroked your hair. Even her naming lacked tenderness. My dad, his siblings, and all the spouses referred to her as "Mother" (not Mom, Mama, or Mommy), and the grandchildren followed suit by calling her "Grandmother." Her maiden name was Cramp, and she lived up to her big-boned, Depression-era practicality and German ancestry.

For whatever reason, she hated her son-in-law, my Uncle Charles. At least that's how my childhood memory recollects it. She picked on him, provoked him, criticizing him for the most minor of grievances. Pure pettiness. Perhaps it was because Uncle Charles married her daughter, my Aunt Brenda and, according to my dad, my grandfather's only daughter and favorite child. Perhaps for some reason my grandmother felt threatened by him, or maybe she found in him an easy target. He is a brilliant yet often absent-minded professor emeritus of applied mathematics, who likes to get lost in solving math equations that, emerging from an old dot matrix printer, run the length of the living room. But I think what really irked her was his ability to ignore her. While the adults cleaned up the kitchen after dinner, my grandmother spewed meanness about my uncle while he was standing there washing *her* dishes. Who does that and then has the audacity to darken the door of a church the following day?

After my mom got the courage to finally transform her naturally brown shoulder-length hair with a box of Clairol semi-wavy hair permanent, my grandmother called her a witch in the presence of family and neighbors. I believe her exact phrase was, "Well, don't you look like a witch!" I was probably only eight or nine years old at the time, but I viscerally felt my mother's embarrassment. Penetrating eyes on you to see how you'll react. We had just arrived after a long drive, and without even getting out of her chair to greet us, that's the first thing that came out of my grandmother's mouth—not hello, or glad to see you, or how was the drive? Perhaps folks were in shock, but I doubt it, since my grandmother got away with saying just about anything she liked. Nobody in that company of witnesses came to my mother's defense except me. In addition to my audible gasp, I told my grandmother that was a horrible thing to say. And the adults who finally did say something only tried to minimize the awkwardness by laughing it off. Even with her granddaughter's public rebuke, or perhaps *because of it*, my grandmother never apologized.

After the birth of my daughter, she came to visit for a few days. As was my custom because of training from my own mother, I doted on my grandmother by bringing her tea, clearing her dishes when she finished eating, and offering her some of her favorite desserts—all fine examples of hospitality. But my grandmother saw it differently. It was then that she said how nice it was to have a "slave." That stopped me in my tracks. Why on earth did she choose that word when there are so many other less in-flammatory terms to convey what I hope she was trying to say—words such as "helper" or "assistant"? Was she really that ignorant? Should I excuse her because she's old and a product of her generation? My guess is she never really concerned herself about racial topics, especially within our American context, with its history of slavery, because she didn't need to. But the second time she called me a "slave," I sat down next to her and firmly explained that I served her out of love and respect for my elders, and certainly not because I was her property and therefore obliged to do so. She never apologized, but she never called me that again.

Because my father participated in the Reserve Officers' Training Corps (ROTC) program while a student at the University of Delaware, he was beholden to the U.S. Army after he completed his graduate studies. Around the year 1968, my father's first tour of active duty was "unaccompanied," which meant family members were not listed on the orders and therefore were not expected to join the service member at the next duty station. While my dad traveled by himself to Bangkok, Thailand, my mother, with my sister in tow, went to live half the year with her parents and the other half with her in-laws. My sister was a toddler at the time, and so my mother felt it important to share equal time with both sets of grandparents. During her six months with my dad's parents, my grandmother also called my mother a "slave," but unlike me, Mom never defended herself, nor did she tell her husband who was half a world away. Perhaps if she had, my grandmother would have known better than to call me dehumanizing names.

My grandmother also had a heart for missions. She sewed sleeping bags for the homeless as well as knitted hats, mittens, and scarves. According to the story my father told me, before their move from Alaska back to the U.S. mainland when they were kids, my grandmother made my Aunt Brenda give away her beloved doll collection. I'm sure there were practical reasons like shipping one fewer box, but my grandmother's main argument revolved around Christian charity. Since the local kids living in isolated Kodiak, Alaska, didn't have access and most likely the funds necessary to acquire the dolls in her collection, my Aunt Brenda needed to give away her prized possessions as a gift to those less fortunate. When I asked my cousin if she had heard this story about her mom, her version went like this: My aunt had received a very special doll, one that came with various accessories, that she specifically requested for Christmas. But within a few weeks after the holiday, she was told to pack up the doll to give to someone else. No matter whether Brenda gave away one doll or the entire collection, the same sentiment remains. She loved all of her dolls, named each one and played with them in her imaginary world for hours. In spite of a young girl's love and attachment to her most favored possessions, undoubtedly birthday and Christmas gifts to her over the years, those were not reasons enough to let her keep them, according to my grandmother.

As a widow, my grandmother fell prey to a phone scammer. She wired a healthy portion of her meager life's savings to strangers over the phone hoping her "investment" would soon guarantee millions to help missionaries around the globe. I always found her motivation to help missionaries in foreign lands a curious passion when some of her own grandchildren were food insecure and living paycheck to paycheck. Or the volume of $5 checks she sent each month to various, and often questionable, mail solicitation charities when she lived on a fixed income. Could she not see the needs in her own backyard? Charity, to my grandmother, does not begin at home because Jesus said, "It is more blessed to give than to receive" (Acts 20:35).

I can't image my grandfather remaining silent about my grandmother's tongue. I'm sure he talked with her; at least I hope he tried. For their children's sake, for my father's sake. However, in the twenty-some years that I knew my grandmother, I saw little evidence that any accountability made much of a difference. And the few altercations I had with my grandmother pale in comparison to the stories my dad and his siblings could tell but don't. Families always have more stories hidden and tucked away. How did my dad survive living under her roof? How did he reconcile my grandfather's sermons about God's love each Sunday with his mother's daily verbal and emotional abuse? Moreover, how did he reconcile the Christian mandate to love unencumbered when the love he witnessed came with limitations and conditions?

Grace, I imagine. And probably some boundaries, too. (Or perhaps the lack thereof.) Everyone knows the behavior of the children is a direct reflection of the parents—a universal phenomenon that has transcended the generational test of time. For my grandparents as leaders in the church, the pressure to model perfect Christian parenthood in the eyes of fellow parishioners must have been stifling. But with the unspoken rule that pastor's kids must exhibit an even higher standard of virtuous living and Christian responsibility, both inside and outside of the church, meant the expectation placed upon the heads of the children was downright suffocating. Sit up straight, stop fidgeting, pay attention, and for goodness' sake, tuck in your shirt and comb your hair.

My dad recalls the story about an indelible moment from his childhood. On the ride to church one morning, my grandmother was irritated and bickering with her four squirmy children. My guess is they were late to church. In my dad's infinite wisdom and youthful cockiness, he suggested they all sing "Jesus Loves Me." Without skipping a beat or cocking her head, my grandmother whipped the back of her hand over the backseat with the intention of smacking my dad across the face. As the eldest of four children, my father was strong enough to grab his mother's wrist in mid-air, and held it there, marking the last time she would lay a hand on him.

Later, when he was a student at the University of Delaware, my father started attending an Episcopal church. I wonder if this transition was willful defiance on my father's part, or merely an attempt to reconcile the mixed-messages of his youth. I image the liturgy presented him with a new style of worship and a fresh interpretation of God's love—a journey that moved him farthest away from his Baptist roots without crossing over the Tiber all the way to Rome. My grandmother found my dad's *Book of Common Prayer* while he was home on break. She said it would "break your dad's heart," but knowing my grandfather, I think it really just broke hers.

Together my parents made the decision to make different choices in managing relationships and child rearing. They also made a conscious decision to radically love my grandmother by showering her with kindness when the path of least resistance was to walk away. In spite of her, they never abandoned the woman who left a trail of hurt and permanent scars in her wake. She did slowly soften with age, and I often wonder if that was a direct result of my parents' constancy or the fact that the river of meanness just finally dried up.

It's a miracle I loved my grandmother. I attribute my love for her to my father, who consciously broke the cycle. In spite of her emotional and verbal abuses, I saw my father treat her with patience. He did not return her behavior with retribution, nor was there any evidence of "eye for an eye." I know this, because my father never called me names.

3

I Saw Something, So I Said Something

If you are neutral in situations of injustice, you have chosen the side of the oppressor.

—Archbishop Desmond Tutu

When Michelle Obama delivered her Democratic National Convention keynote speech in 2020, and spoke the following words, I swear she was speaking directly to me:

> Echoing heroes like John Lewis, who said, "When you see something that is not right, you must say something. You must do something." That is the truest form of empathy. Not just feeling, but doing. Not just for ourselves, or our kids but for everyone. For all our kids.[1]

For someone who had felt helpless since the 2016 election, I grappled with how one White, straight, middle-aged woman could make a difference. I was just an ordinary housewife after all, so what on earth could I contribute to make this world a better place? The day after Trump won, I joined the American Civil Liberties Union (ACLU) and made a contribution to Covenant House, a charity that shelters homeless youth. I also bought a fundraising T-shirt with oversized letters spelling out "Reject Hate." Yet I knew real boots-on-the-ground-change that goes well beyond

1. Obama, "Transcript: Michelle Obama," lines 107–9.

donations and T-shirts begins with me. But how? In the midst of the COV-ID-19 pandemic, I wouldn't join the throngs of people protesting because, well, I could contract the disease, spread it, and die. And then it dawned on me: My life is so comfortable that I don't have to risk anything. I could opt out of participating in a critical political protest for social change during a pandemic because I didn't have to—*my life did not depend on it.*

Instead, I spent time listening to Black narratives—who better to ask than primary sources. The first eye-opener right out of the gate was the validity of Black Lives Matter (BLM). My parents refused to endorse this ideology since they misinterpreted the slogan to mean "*only* Black Lives Matter" or "Black Lives Matter *more than other lives.*" Instead of adopting a "Black Lives Matter *too*" mentality, they preferred to respond with the popular rebuttal: "All Lives Matter." *Of course* all lives matter, but the point is we can't celebrate *all* until every person outside the fold is accounted for and fully accepted within the larger community.

I'd like to know how my parents justify "All Lives Matter" with the parable of the lost sheep. In his parable, Jesus doesn't provide a checklist before the search to see if the lost sheep fits a certain criterion. The only condition is that the sheep is lost. It is enough that the sheep is unprotected and vulnerable, and as such, is already worthy of being found. And neither does he say anything about the remaining ninety-nine—not because they are less valuable—but because he doesn't have to. It is understood that the ninety-nine haven't been abandoned or disenfranchised or cast out. They are not the ones in danger.[2]

But a sheep is a sheep is a sheep. So, what happens to the parable when we make it less about the abstract and replace the sheep with something more concrete? For example, what if that one lost sheep were a Black man? Or a transgender youth? Or a Muslim seeking asylum? Or a gay pastor? Does Jesus' teaching only apply if the sheep looks and acts just like the other ninety-nine?

---

2. Price, "If you are a Christian," Facebook, May 31, 2020.

David Hayward, aka NakedPastor, "All Sheep Matter." Used by permission.

The current debate with my family, following the Minneapolis protests in May 2020 after the murder of George Floyd at the hands of a police officer who knelt on Floyd's neck for nine minutes and twenty-nine seconds until he suffocated, revolved around protesting and why protesters loot. My father specifically asked, "What good does protesting achieve?" I quickly reminded him that in 1971, a bunch of high school kids protested on Capitol Hill to change the voting age to eighteen. It took them more than a decade, but they succeeded. And it was no coincidence that all those women wearing pink "pussy" hats, who flooded Constitution Avenue in protest after Trump's election, encouraged scores of women who not only ran for public office but also who won. Marches and protests work.

But my family's narrative went something like this: if Black people really cared about protesting and making a difference, they wouldn't destroy property in the process. Generally speaking, our collective social contract says that destroying property, stealing, and therefore looting is wrong. So, why do some people do it? A valid question for which, I too, wanted an explanation.

After Colin Kaepernick, former quarterback for the San Francisco 49ers, took a knee in 2016 in protest against racism in our country, my father left that football season just like Vice President Pence. Kaepernick used his professional football platform to reach millions of viewers through a peaceful protest of solidarity for fellow Americans experiencing social injustices in our communities. However, my dad, who played center on the University of Delaware's football team and later served in the military, couldn't get past Kaepernick taking advantage of America's favorite pastime to disrespect our flag and National Anthem.

As a kid growing up on a military base, I knew the respect owed to our American flag and anthem. If I was riding my bike at Ft. Detrick, Maryland around 4:30pm and heard taps through the megaphones, I knew to stop and get off my bike. With the lowering of the flag "in retreat" after the day's activities, I faced the flag with my hand over my heart. Even service men and women driving on the base would stop their cars in the middle of the road, get out, and salute the lowering flag. Life pauses so we can take a minute to honor the American flag, our proud symbol of freedom. To this day, I don't take my eyes off the flag during the national anthem at sporting events, and I've been known to tell people around me to show the same respect.

My dad, however, totally missed the point. Kaepernick wasn't burning the flag or saluting with the middle finger, he was simply taking a knee. The point was to shock us out of complacency, to bend the body because words alone for the last four hundred years have barely made a dent. And if my father had bothered to discover Kaepernick's motivations by really listening to him, he'd find that Kaepernick actually loves and respects this country—*just like he does*. Kaepernick was willing to be a mouthpiece speaking with a symbolic gesture that says he can't literally stand for "the land of the free" until *all* Americans are treated equitably. And he practiced what he preached because he was willing to lose his job for it. If athletes taking a knee is disrespectful, what then is the proper way to protest racism, according to my White father? More specifically, if a peaceful protest like taking a knee is shunned, what method should the Black community use to articulate crimes against them?

I found two video clips that helped answer my question about looting. The first clip is by Trevor Noah, the South African comedian and host of *The Daily Show*. During COVID even TV studios streamed remotely, so Trevor, wearing a sweatshirt and seated in his living room, departs from comedy and addresses looting. His argument is simple. A successful society is based on an unspoken contract in which all of its citizens must agree on a set of "common rules, common ideals, and common practices."[3] Most citizens will abide by the contract no matter their social and economic standing within the group. But others will break it. Why? According to Noah, minorities often break the contract by looting because they figure, *why not?* Time and time again the Black community has witnessed unchecked or poorly prosecuted police brutality and murder, so "there is no contract if the law and people in power don't uphold their end of it."[4] Since the contract they signed doesn't protect them equally, it's not surprising they no longer have a vested interest in playing by the rules.

The second video clip is by Kimberly Jones, co-author of the book *I'm Not Dying with You Tonight*. While interviewing George Floyd protestors in Atlanta, she recorded a short video entitled "How Can We Win?" about racism which subsequently went viral. In her outlet, she uses the analogy of Monopoly to explain America's race problem: Imagine we play a game of Monopoly, but I don't have any money to get on the board to buy houses and hotels, and after working tirelessly I finally earn enough to buy some real estate, yet you decide to take my money and my property anyway. Jones points out, "That was Tulsa. That was Rosewood. Those are places where we built Black economic wealth, we were self-sufficient, where we owned our stores, where we owned our property, and they [White mobs] burned them to the ground."[5]

While not perfect, the analogies of a social contract and a game of Monopoly clicked for me because my love language is fairness. Childhood tantrums come to mind when, all of a sudden, my winning basket or slide into home plate was suddenly null and void because my opponent decided to change the rules mid-game. Or conversely, when I knew the strategy of how to win at the board game Othello, yet purposefully did not tell my

3. Noah, "George Floyd," March 29, 2020.
4. Noah, "George Floyd," March 29, 2020.
5. Jones, "How Can We Win?," June 9, 2020.

opponent who was just learning the game. She never could beat me, at least not until an adult had mercy and told her to aim for the corners. I can also distinctly remember telling my own children that before playing any game, make sure everyone involved agrees on the rules.

But my experience of fairness and rules-following is mere child's play when compared to the racism on full display in both videos. There is nothing in my upbringing or life's experiences that allows me to feel the pain, suffering, and injustice that Black Americans have endured at the hands of White people. *Nothing.* I was so taken by the "ah-ha" moment of these monologues that I shared them on Facebook, but the idea that I actually could change someone's mind by posting these videos on social media is as preposterous as it is naïve to think that folks would actually watch them. I was hopeful, however, that my earnestness could sway because certainly they, too, must be as troubled by our divided nation as I was. Plant the seed, I thought. If they cared, moreover, if they respected me, they would watch. While one White friend commented on my post so she could find it for later, she never did follow up. Another acquaintance, who happened to a Black woman, earnestly thanked me.

At the time I really didn't understand the price of what "saying something" might cost, especially since for all of my life I haven't had to say anything. I've never confessed the following story to anyone except my cousin. I vacillate between feeling embarrassed about the whole ordeal and wanting to avoid the impending scorn from my family, so in the end, I decide not to poison the well.

Several of my aunts, uncles, and cousins participate in Facebook and other social media platforms. It's been a great vehicle to stay connected, especially during COVID, when a spring break trip to visit Aunt Marie and Uncle Pete in Arizona got cancelled. We anticipated hiking, discovering the desert topography and cactus blooms, and most importantly, partaking in my aunt's amazing cooking. As a full-blooded Italian, she is the type of aunt who insists that your stomach remain full and you lack nothing. I was happy to oblige.

Well before the pandemic shutdown, I got a phone call from my uncle, a former pharmaceutical executive, asking us not to come because they needed to protect my aunt's compromised health at all cost. As a scientist, he could fathom the potential danger ahead that the rest of the world could not. In fact, they didn't attend their son's remarriage later that summer knowing the risk was too great—a restraint for my aunt that must have meant moving heaven and earth.

Aunt Marie, an active Facebook member who regularly commented on my posts about my kids, posted a graphic that caught my attention. At first glance, it seemed humorous and innocuous, so I kept scrolling. But for some reason, it just didn't sit well with me, so I kept ruminating on it until I was able to place my finger on why. A couple days later, when I eventually put it all together, the brunt of the joke made a sly correlation about COVID, minorities, and looting. I started to type a response to my aunt, but then rapidly hit the delete key. Michelle Obama was right when she said "saying something" would be difficult.

I eventually responded by reattaching the Trevor Noah video about looting and asked her to think about her post differently. Aunt Marie reacted swiftly and with great passion telling me I make everything political, and besides, she was just trying to make people smile. "But at whose expense?" I asked, adding, "You can unfriend me if you like, but I'm not going to stay silent." Her last words to me were "Get over it!" And that was that. By the time I went back to take a screen shot of the meme, our exchange disappeared into thin air. She had permanently blocked me.

My initial response involved sending them a short apology via email. Social media is useless as a vehicle for engaging in meaningful conversations; a letter or phone call would have been better. And yes, I knew better. But I was confused because I felt certain that my aunt, herself a grandmother to three half-Filipino children, would be interested in racial issues. What hurt the most, though, was that her response told me she didn't care about the injustices that perhaps even her own biracial grandchildren have experienced. She wasn't interested in learning about racism and how we got here because in her mind her good intentions were enough. It didn't matter how many casualties fell by the wayside as long as her feel-good post reached its intended audience—her like-minded friends and family.

I am fully aware that my aunt blocking me on Facebook is rather trivial, especially when people have lost far more over much less. Any time a door slams on a relationship, though, there is sadness. Some people might say I should have minded my own business. Who the hell do I think I am that I should ask my aunt to do better, to be better? Is it my job to point out another person's racism? All valid questions.

But what happens when we ask it a different way like "Who is my neighbor?"[6]

Even after several months, I couldn't shake this unsettling exchange with my aunt, and I even lost sleep over my actions. But why? My discontent went so much deeper than simply identifying my aunt's racism on Facebook and being blocked for it. Yes, I called out her insensitive and hurtful post *in a public space*. Yes, I tried to point out that the nameless dark-skinned, COVID-infected looting person she made fun of in the meme *is her neighbor*. And yes, I so desperately wanted her *to care*. Instead, she slammed the door on me. So why, on earth, did I feel *I had to apologize* to her? My aunt is the one who showed her true colors—why, then, am I carrying the guilt and shame?

Because "blessed are the peacemakers."[7]

My first attempt to really "say something," even something this inconsequential on social media, taught me something far greater than I ever anticipated. All my life I have been taught that it is my job as a Christian woman to calm the waters, to seek reconciliation, to mend. Similarly, I should avoid offending at all costs. Be hospitable. Make others comfortable. Be encouraging, not outspoken. Stay quiet—that is the Christian response—because making a scene and calling people out are divisive behaviors and not fruits of the Spirit. Most importantly, be a calming presence because God, in the end, will judge the wicked.

While some will see my actions with my aunt as stirring the pot, the irony is, *I was being a peacemaker*. I see that now. I was trying to reconcile my aunt with the poor soul at the butt of her joke. I wanted her to see the human being at the core of her post and empathize. Even though he was a stranger, I was willing to speak up for him. And I am so proud I did.

I regret now that I asked my aunt for an apology. I was not wrong to call her out, nor was I wrong to do it on social media. I would even argue that the rift that opened between us was not initiated by my action, but by her dehumanizing post. It is never wrong to stand up for the disenfranchised and the oppressed. Uncomfortable, yes. But never wrong.

Despite my failure to change my aunt's thinking, I'm hopeful my comments planted a seed. I'm hopeful that when my aunt is confronted

6. Luke 10:29.
7. Matt 5:9.

again, and my guess is she will be, that the seed of discontent grows until she can no longer ignore it. If we hear it or see it and we walk away, we are part of the problem. In fact, we are partners in crime who conspire together to continue the dehumanizing narrative. To say nothing speaks volumes because our silence actually says we consent, and this gives power back to the oppressor. If you hear something, *say something*. Every. Damn. Time. Even on Facebook.

4

The Floodgate

You own everything that happened to you. Tell your stories. If people wanted you to write warmly about them, they should have behaved better.

—Anne Lamott

S ince my father's no-politics-at-the-Thanksgiving-table edict, my family members have exchanged little more beyond pleasantries and general inquiries—"How are the kids?"—and discussions about plans for our annual family beach vacation. I know this because all modern methods of communication leave a trail of breadcrumbs. For example, I went back into my email account and catalogued all the politically motivated emails I sent my parents—roughly fifty-five between October 2017 and January 2021. Surprisingly fewer than I thought.

The number leading up to The Floodgate: Zero.

In May of 2017, six months after Trump's election, my parents came to North Carolina to participate in my daughter's confirmation, a formal rite of passage in the Episcopal Church. Because we believe in infant baptism, confirmation provides the opportunity for baptized teens and adults to publicly "express a mature commitment to Christ."[1] There is a yearlong curriculum around this event, including lessons about the prayers and liturgy and how the church "works." The local bishop also comes and lays

1. *Book of Common Prayer*, 860.

hands on each candidate, thus consecrating this event in the eyes of the church and larger community. In addition, each candidate has a sponsor who commits to supporting him/her/them through the journey. My daughter chose my mother, the Rev. Jean Alexander.

One of my favorite pictures of my mom is an impromptu snapshot of us at the beach when I was probably three or four years old. My mom is sitting high on the chiseled rocks with my sister and me below her on either side. Together, our postures create the perfect triangle. She's wearing one of those fabulous, modest floral bikinis with the high-waisted bottom that accentuates her long, lean legs. The ocean breezes lift the hair around her face, and she gazes piercingly into the camera. Even though the photo paper has faded into sepia tones, you can see her bronze skin and freckles dotting her nose. She is gorgeous. And I swear she could have been Jackie Kennedy Onassis' cousin. My dad longingly refers to that era as her "bohemian days," when she drove with the windows down and didn't care about messing up her beehive.

But that was not the mother of my adolescence. The '80s were different times, where modesty morphed into string bikinis and midriffs. Once I came of age, I was forbidden from wearing a bikini to the pool. And blue jeans, or dungarees as she often called them, were off limits for school. I'm sure my mother's obsession with what her children—*her daughters*—wore in public had everything to do with her growing up poor. My mother might have been wearing hand-me-downs in her grammar school pictures, but you'd never know it. My mom's mother, affectionately known as Nana, was a fur coat window model for an upscale department store before she married my grandfather. Nana understood the importance of blouses and pleated skirts ironed neatly in place in the attempt to fit into a class above her means. As soon as you leave the house, appearances meant everything. That philosophy did not skip my mother's generation.

My mom was always forthright about wanting to raise her daughters into strong women. I'm just not exactly sure what she meant by "strong," nor how wearing a bikini might alter that goal. I imagine it was a combination of coming out of the '60s and into the women's rights movement. No, my mother has never been a feminist, and she bristles at the label, but I do feel she wanted us to be successful in careers and marriage. In my case, I think she got more than she bargained for.

My mother came into the Episcopal priesthood as a second career when I was an undergraduate student. She had been a registered nurse for many years and, through working in hospice, discovered she had a different calling to formal ordained ministry. I also think she decided long before her ordination journey began to seek some sort of religious vocation when my father showed little interest or conviction in taking on the traditional role of "spiritual head of the household." We did not grow up with family devotions, so it felt odd when out-of-the-blue Mom rallied the troops one evening to gather in the living room. But once Dad had an audience, it was awkward and he was visibly uncomfortable—like being forced to wear a suit two sizes too small. But my mom is a natural. Even before putting on the collar, she had a knack for turning something benign into a spiritual nugget—like transforming the gift of a solar lantern into "spreading the light of Christ." No matter her vocation, though, she wouldn't seek ordination unless she had the blessing of her entire family since "a house divided against itself cannot stand. . . ."[2]

Lest she get swallowed in the belly of the whale like Jonah, who tried to flee God's calling to serve, Mom patiently worked with the longest holdout, my brother-in-law, who believed at the time that Jesus drank grape juice (not wine) and that women shouldn't preach to or teach men. I remember that conversation like it was yesterday. While sitting in the front parlor of our turn-of-the-century Sears and Roebuck house, my brother-in-law challenged my mother, a seminary student at the time, about whether or not the "wine" of the Bible was really just watered-down grape juice. My brother-in-law, who accepted Jesus in college and adopted, among other things, teetotaling Southern Baptist ideology, wanted further confirmation that modern-day Christians should abstain from alcohol. Thankfully, at some point along his journey, he did make peace with Jesus drinking wine and enjoys a glass himself.

In the Episcopal tradition, women are not limited to positions of choir directors and Sunday school teachers, traditional female roles in most evangelical churches and many Protestant denominations. Since the Episcopal Church first ordained women in 1974, I grew up seeing ordained women priests baptize babies, preach from the pulpit, and serve Communion. In fact, that's all I knew. It wasn't until my freshman year at Wheaton College in Illinois, when I took the required "Christian Thought" class, that I first encountered the idea that women weren't "supposed" to preach. I was the only one in the classroom half puzzled and half bemused because my fellow students felt there was something to debate.

2. Matt 12:25.

I don't regret attending an evangelical college, the same institution that graduated Billy Graham decades earlier (but refused admission to his son, Franklin, even after it christened one of the main buildings on campus after the elder Graham). While I was one of perhaps a couple dozen Episcopalians in the student body in the late 1980s, it was the right place for me at the time because there is certain safety in conservatism. I wasn't the partying type. I've never smoked a cigarette in my life, nor did I take drugs, or drink as a minor. I was a virgin until my wedding night. I could have attended Boston University, but the sock hanging on the dorm room doorknob during my campus tour steered me clear. Touted as the "Harvard among small liberal arts Christian colleges" by *U.S. News and World Report* in the '80s, Wheaton lived up to its reputation. Professors taught me to think and to write, and to see the world through a "Christian lens," but not to be blinded by it. I was introduced to books and authors and ideas that challenged me and opened my worldview. I met my husband there, and together we have maintained strong friendships to this day with several fellow classmates.

After our first date, I knew I could marry someone like Jeff. We met in Dr. Joel Sheesley's art survey class in Blanchard Hall, the iconic tower on campus built in 1853 which later served as a stop in the Underground Railroad. After our class field trip to the Art Institute of Chicago, Jeff walked me back to my dorm and asked me out on a date. But when Jeff tells the story, he'll tell you it was the "Naked and the Nude" lecture that brought us together. He is a gregarious, kind, and thoughtful person, and even to this day keeps programs and ticket stubs from our adventures. He's sentimental like that. He strolled up to my dorm that evening of our first date wearing a blue seersucker jacket with pressed khaki pants, red bow tie, white suede bucks, and swinging an umbrella. He proudly displayed his Southern roots, but aside from his charm and dapperness, what really caught my attention was he knew where he was going in life. He had a plan, and thankfully, I was part of it.

And that really is the crux of college life—the relationships built while living in a microcosm. The late Roger Lundin, a Wheaton professor and scholar of early American literature, was a legend in the field and a gentle giant whose intellect nevertheless intimidated the crap out of me. We read *Moby Dick*, poetry by Anne Bradstreet, and the sermon "Sinners in the Hands of an Angry God" by Jonathan Edwards. I remember nothing of those lectures. But I do recall vividly his lecture about the histories and intertwined timelines shared by siblings. Lundin wept in class over the death of his brother, lamenting that the only person in the world who could relate to his history and reminisce about shared memories was gone. When that chapter closed in Lundin's life, it ushered in great sadness and isolation. That is, he said, until he learned to share his history through story—something each of us can do—bringing his lecture back to the power of words and books. I was hooked.

I, too, have one sibling. I can't say that we were exactly best friends growing up. She is four years older and five years ahead of me in school, but I am a quarter-inch taller. The one year we overlapped in elementary school, we walked to school together, but my sister, who was faster, wouldn't wait for me. I'm the one who had to catch up. I don't have memories of us playing together as children. She is outgoing; I am shy. We fought. And she certainly didn't want me participating in anything having to do with her friends. I basically didn't feel a deeply rooted connection to her until she left for college, when the void of her physical presence taught me to appreciate her. Ever since, she is the first person I call when I have good news or bad. She provides the glitter to my practicality. She is the Queen of Returns, and I am the Decisive One. And our ongoing competition involves who can find the biggest bargain on the clearance shelf. So far, she holds the record with foiled Christmas wrapping paper at twenty-five cents per roll.

While I got an excellent education, college was also one of the loneliest times of my life, largely because I didn't know how or where to fit in. I was the proverbial fish out of water. During my undergraduate years, I never found a church home, and so bounced between churches of various denominations throughout my college career. If I attended an Episcopal service, I wouldn't see any of my peers from the college; if I went with the majority of the student body to College Church on the corner of campus, it was a religious tradition I didn't recognize. Eventually, these experiences sealed my love of the liturgy and my home in the Episcopal Church. I love the movement and structure and repetition of the service, the liturgical calendar with symbolic colors that shift with the seasons: purple for Advent and Lent, red for Pentecost, and white for festival days such as Christmas and Easter. The constancy of the Prayers of the People, the Nicene Creed, and the Apostles' Creed connects us to the early church and echoes the voices of saints long gone. The notion that millions of Episcopalians and Anglicans around the world worship with the same liturgy and in every language gives me pause. I love that our human-generated sermons, shorter than in most other Christian denominations, are secondary in importance to Communion, a spiritual rite practiced in most American Episcopal churches every Sunday and not just on special days.

And what I appreciate most is that Episcopalians don't claim to have all the answers; instead, we ask questions, tough questions. We think and wrestle. We confess our doubts and celebrate the mystery. Moreover, our quest to answer these questions doesn't stop with *for the Bible tells me so*; instead, we cast a very wide net across religious, political, social, and intellectual scholarship. We don't drink from a single well.

Ironically, all of the local Episcopal churches near the college were loaded with Wheaton faculty members, yet the pews were largely devoid of Wheaton students. Dr. Joe Hill McClatchey, a favored English professor and an ordained Episcopal priest who died of cancer in 1991 at the age of fifty-five before I could take his legendary Modern Mythology class, regularly held Vespers, Evening Prayer, at the chapel next to the Cloud Room in the Billy Graham Center. "All are Welcome," he would say. I brought a friend with me once who was completely confused by the liturgy, something sweet and familiar I so desperately needed. My four years at college gave me a window into conservative Christian thought and theology, but from the unique vantage point from my "liberal" Episcopal religious experience. Unlike most college experiences, my view through a wide-angle lens changed to telephoto, not as a permanent transformation, but as a necessary one.

Since my mother's ordination in 1995, her preaching has become second nature. She studies and writes and reads. She loves to preach, and her truest calling is to local outreach and global missions. She genuinely loves the people she serves—all the people. During my father's tour of duty in Panama from 1980 to 1983, my mother frequented Palo Seco, the leper colony and hospital just west of the Panama Canal's Pacific Ocean entrance. She knew each patient there by first name, learned their stories, and tried her best to mitigate their isolation through friendship. I visited, too, on occasion, especially when musicians from our church brought their guitars to lead praise and worship songs. Despite the music, the walls were steeped in sadness since many patients had family nearby who refused to visit. One visit in particular stands out in my memory. When we arrived, there was a car loaded with family of all ages. But they were just sitting there in the car. As my mother and I rounded the parking lot, I saw the driver vomiting by the side of the car. My mother explained that the pain of the lepers' suffering is often too great for many people.

While she is a priest of the Episcopal Church, with all the "smells and bells" of liturgical processions, my mom is still, in many ways, a small "b" baptist. For example, despite the Episcopal tradition of infant baptism, my parents did not baptize me and my sister as babies because of hold-over Baptist theology that dictated personal choice in professions of faith. Mom would tell you she regrets that decision now because God's grace is always present whether we accept it or not. The global Anglican Church, of which the Episcopal Church in the United States is a part, like every other Christian church tradition, includes members who hold a spectrum of theological beliefs, from conservative to progressive. The irony is my mother has a foot in both ends. Her ability as a woman to be a priest with full rights and privileges rests on the shoulders of progressives who broke through the stained-glass ceiling of gender bias and discrimination. Yet twice she chose to work under a White male priest, whose conservatism most closely aligned with hers, and who excluded her from the regular preaching rota on account of her gender.

I, too, have found myself straddling the same fence. After my daughter started kindergarten, I decided to go back to work. Holding a master's degree in English but without a teaching certificate, I could teach only in private schools. And with a limited number of such schools in the area, and even fewer with openings in the English department, when I saw a position at Trinity Christian School in Fairfax, Virginia, I leapt at the opportunity. A Wheaton diploma will open just about every evangelical door, especially when the head of school is an alumnus. The crazy thing is, after I interviewed in person and toured the school, the head of school walked me out to my car and handed me a blue folder with a hot-off-the-press contract inside. There was no waiting period, no follow-up interviews, no "we'll be in touch." I was elated, but I should have been suspicious. While the interview process was smooth, I had no idea the giant ideological foe that awaited me.

I was not concerned about working at a Christian school, since after all, I am a practicing Christian myself. Surely such a school would embrace diversity of thought in the student body as well as the faculty. We were a rigorous learning institution, after all. I'm pretty sure I was the only faculty member who voted for Obama twice, and without a doubt, I was the only one whose mother was an Episcopal priest, a fact I openly celebrated. I was okay with stirring the pot, being different, and challenging others to see Christianity differently—a bifurcation of my overall vocation. I opened my class not with prayer but with a resounding Episcopal refrain: "The Lord be with you." My students quickly learned to respond, "And also with you." In the end, however, I was no match for this Goliath.

I was tough on my students—not unkind, but demanding. My first exposure to teaching English was at Westover School, one of the few all-girls boarding schools nestled in the pastoral rolling hills of rural Connecticut. We were in league with Miss Porter's, Avon Old Farms, and Choate Rosemary Hall, powerhouse schools that put kids on the map and into the Ivy League. My bar was pretty high. My Trinity students inherited the same lessons, a mixture of lecture notes from my undergraduate and graduate classes and fine-tuned expository literature notes from my esteemed Westover colleagues. For example, my students didn't just read Chaucer's Canterbury Tales, they experienced it. I expected my students to recite the first eighteen lines of the prologue, in Middle English, from memory, and in front of their peers. Why? So, they could own a piece of our linguistic history—and, of course, some day impress their boss at the company office party, I joked. In the end, the students were proud of their accomplishment, and the exercise bolstered their confidence.

I was especially hard on their writing. I worked tirelessly on exercises to show the need for transitions, and how to use them effectively. We worked on sentence structure, sentence variety, and organization of ideas. We practiced writing a thesis and supporting topic sentences. I also gave them copious notes on their essays and looked for implementation of my suggestions in their future work. If the support for their thesis was lacking, I told them so. "A's" were earned and hard to come by.

During our daily faculty devotions before the school day, the head of school delivered his thoughts on that morning's Scripture lesson. On this morning, his demeanor, usually serious and intense, showed a thread of anger. Some days he had a knack for weaving faculty offenses publicly into his devotions to see if folks were paying attention, but mainly as a warning shot. This was one of those mornings. Instead of pulling me aside to address my infraction, as Scripture commands, he chose to wield his power and humiliate me in public in front of my peers. No, he didn't name names. He also never asked for my side of the story. I was convinced right then that there would be a special ring in hell for this type of school administrator who found satisfaction in publicly shaming an employee because he didn't have the balls to talk with her in person.

During exams the previous week, a woman, whose husband was on the board of directors, was waiting for me with her son's English paper in hand. As soon as I opened my classroom door, I saw her, but continued giving final instructions to my students, fielding questions from them, and collecting their exams as they shot out the door. It was chaotic and stressful. I eventually acknowledged her, at which point she handed me her son's paper and asked me to take another look. I handed the paper back to her and told her I'd be happy to discuss this with her, but she'd need to set up an appointment. My guess is she didn't take kindly to that and stormed off to the head of school's office to give him an earful. But when I was summoned to his office at three o'clock on a Friday afternoon later that spring, a symphony of alarm bells should have gone off in my mind. He was not renewing my contract, he said, because I was too hard, the hand-picked students he talked to in the hallways didn't like me or my class, and my electives had low enrollment. It didn't matter one iota that I received a highly complementary teaching evaluation a few weeks prior, because tuition-driven schools always side with the parents. With tears steadily streaming down my cheeks, I was forced to walk the path of shame from his office across campus, through the congested carpool line filled with parents picking up their children, and back to the protection of my classroom.

My father reminded me of his favorite mantra that "cooler heads prevail." The following Monday, after much anguish and thought, I calmly turned in my letter of resignation. Then I told each one of my classes I was leaving. I wanted them to hear it directly from me and on my terms. My student Alexis, who I still keep up with on social media, was so upset she sought me out to ask if it was really true. I agonized over what that would mean for her and all of my students, but in the end, I couldn't continue to work for an institution that had no confidence in me. Had I stayed, I would have just been a warm body and *persona non grata* in the faculty lounge. My husband and I had toyed with the idea of moving away from the frenzy of the Washington, DC, metro area. This was just the catalyst we needed. Before school ended for the year, we put our house on the market. Instead of grading exams, I was packing housewares into boxes.

My dad and I were the only family members in the pew the morning of my daughter's confirmation on May 21, 2017. Claire and my mother were lined up with the other candidates, my son was an acolyte, and my husband was rehearsing with the tenor section in the basement of the church. Having arrived early for the event, my dad and I found an empty pew well before the prelude music began. In good church etiquette, it's typical to remain silent so as to quiet the soul in preparation for the service, but because the sanctuary was nearly empty, we spoke in hushed voices. It was there that my dad leaned over and confessed that he couldn't understand why many of his good friends were so upset about his support of Trump.

And there it was—a verbal grenade gently rolled on sacred ground, blowing open six months of bottlenecked political silence that rivaled Milton's Pandemonium.

This was not, however, the first contentious moment with my father while inside of a church. When I was about ten years old and visiting grandparents one summer, we were in the middle of singing an unfamiliar song at church when my father stiffened his back and slammed his hymnal shut. The hymn was about gardening and tending to the flowers, about taking care of God's creation. When my dad's love of dahlias came to mind during the middle of the song, I elbowed him and pointed to the words under the musical scale. Although dahlias produce vibrant blooms, unlike daffodils and tulips, they require extra labor by digging up the bulbs every fall, storing the tubers in a cool dry place, and then replanting them again in the spring. My dad's garden was prizeworthy and a beautiful sight to behold. Stunned by my father's reaction, I, too, stopped singing. My dad had interpreted my gesture as an insult, equating it with all the other times I jeered at him for singing painfully off tune. My dad, just like my grandmother, inherited not only her love of singing but also her ability to sing every note of the musical scale in random order hoping to eventually land on the right one. Yet they both ignored a lifetime of side-eyed glances and subtle half-head-turns from folks near them in the pews, living fully into the Bible's invitation "to make a joyful noise."[3]

Still roiled by my insensitivity, my father marched us out to the car after the service. I was in tears, begging him to listen to my side of the story. I was indeed guilty of criticizing my father's singing in the past, so he was conditioned to react. And I guess this time he'd had enough. Once I explained to him, through sobbing tears, my father's shoulders relaxed. He heard me, and saw the situation for what it was, a big misunderstanding. Children often view parents, who are stoic in their dispositions and emotionally guarded, as impervious to outside influences. The Rock of Gibraltar. And pillars of strength. This event was one of the first allowing me to see my father for who he was—fully human and susceptible to criticism.

3. Ps 100:1.

The day of my daughter's confirmation was quite different, however. Why my father felt it appropriate to open the political hatches right before my daughter's confirmation is beyond me. It was mean, inappropriate, thoughtless, and felt strangely and strategically timed. Or was he just clueless? The symbolism is not lost on me either, since the church is a place of confession and the sanctuary of protection. My guess is he felt safe. It's as if he knew a thorough response from me, one requiring the entire length of the service, would miraculously be delayed with the first blast of the organ. Out of Christian charity, I tried my damnedest to exhibit one final show of restraint, but after the service, all bets were off. To this day, I feel sorry for the poor souls who unknowingly sat near us.

As much as I tried not to let my father's unholy hand grenade ruin such a milestone spiritual moment, all joy was sucked out from that sacred space. It was as if the doors separating church and state were flung open, creating a vacuum, and pulling out anything remotely beautiful. I was numb, but I went through the motions anyway. I said the prayers and mumbled the promises from the liturgy, because they are the same words I've been reciting since before I could read, but my head and my heart weren't in it. I smiled for the pictures, and tried to remain present for my daughter, but internally, I was too far gone. Who exactly is my dad, and what is happening to me?

For months I had dutifully honored my father's Thanksgiving edict by avoiding politics well beyond the holiday because he provided no expiration date. But as news from the Trump White House grew more absurd and chaotic by the day, I became more and more frustrated, agitated even, wondering how my family could act as if nothing was wrong by ignoring the elephant in the room. As I watched the political circus, I wondered what they were thinking and feeling. Is this what they voted for? Were they, in fact, okay with this? Not surprising then, my father's confession at church that confirmation morning gave me just the permission I needed to release the pressure building within me. If my dad really didn't comprehend why his vote for Trump was perplexing to his friends and to me, I was more than prepared to enlighten him. What neither of us anticipated was the rage that came with it.

5

No Rainbow after the Flood

Remind yourself that anger and rage is a valid emotional response
to trauma and injustice.

—@MINAA_B

Since all the nieces and nephews were little, our family has gathered
every summer at the beach for a week. We've rented houses in Virginia
Beach, then migrated as far south as Anna Maria Island in Florida, then
to Kiawah Island and Pawleys Island in South Carolina, but landing predominantly at Topsail Beach, North Carolina. As the family grew, so did
the size of the beach house, and consequently, the rental cost. Every year
we'd schlep beach chairs and strollers from our rental to the beach because
we were too cheap to splurge for ocean front. And then there were meals to
cook for triple the number of people. While I love getting together, beach
week loosely holds the word "vacation" for me.

Now that most of the kids are adults and starting their own lives,
beach trips are getting more difficult, and frankly unrealistic, to plan.
How do we wrangle the schedules of twelve adults to find one week within
the summer months that works for everyone? Another result of having
nearly all adults in the house is having weightier conversations. My niece
and one of my nephews particularly enjoy throwing out a highly contested
topic during the dinner hour, and the subject du jour from the last few
trips has been homosexuality. The younger generation seem genuinely
conflicted about what their conservative leadership has been teaching
them on the subject. Which book, chapter, and verse does Jesus explicitly

condemn homosexuality? And more importantly, what happens if everything they've been taught is wrong?

Since I don't recall having these types of in-depth conversations in my family of origin growing up, it's from these multigenerational table-side discussions that I've learned more fully where my parents stand. And it still amazes me how free-flowing and easy these conversations happen for my family. Everybody has something to say. For example, my mother has been very forthright about her decision not to marry same-sex couples, not because she dislikes them as people (she will tell you many of her friends are gay), but because in her view Scripture does not support it. In 2015, the Episcopal Church opened the sacrament of marriage to include gay couples; however, as a priest she still has the right to refuse to preside at a same-sex wedding and to send the couple to another priest who will. The irony here is that my mother presided at my cousin's wedding even though he had been cohabitating with his girlfriend prior to marriage—still very much a sin in the eyes of the church. The whole extended family knew of their choice to live together, but we were instructed not to talk about their arrangement in front of our grandmother.

Mom is open to changing her mind about marrying a gay couple, she says, but right now her view is the Bible does not support gay marriage. I interjected into the conversation that there is no equivalent for the English word "homosexual" in the Greek or Hebrew lexicon. As a former seminary student, she would know that, too. "Homosexual" is a modern word applying to a concept unknown in the ancient world, including the biblical world—namely, that of a stable same-sex orientation. The Bible never discusses homosexuality because its authors had no awareness of it. Yet the word "homosexual" has been irresponsibly used in some modern English translations of biblical texts describing illicit sexual activity. And in this way, the Bible—a text about unconditional love—has been weaponized against a vulnerable, minority community. When I continued that "homosexual" was only added to the Revised Standard Version of the Bible in 1946, nobody responded. It's as if my comment had no relevance, especially when a new opinion smothered mine and sent the conversation in another direction. I didn't say another word because either no one was listening, or they simply didn't care.

Mom also shared a story in which she says she was aggressively approached by a lesbian. As my mother relayed this very painful and private story, she used predatory language to tell her account. I waited for her to make the disclaimer that not all homosexuals are aggressors, but when that never came, I blurted out, "You can't say that!" While I have no doubt about her justification for feeling the way she did, what I really wanted her to clarify was that as a married woman, *any unwanted advances from anyone*, heterosexual or homosexual, is jarring and offensive. But that never came either.

My dad also shared a revealing antidote about homosexuality. They were facing a dilemma, he explained, about an upcoming wedding. They were anticipating an invitation to the wedding of the child of good friends, and the child is gay. My father openly confessed they struggled with attending the wedding at all because they didn't want to give the impression they condoned same-sex unions. If they decided not to attend, would sending a gift give the same impression, he wondered aloud. As my dad meticulously smoothed the wrinkles of his place mat, an outward sign of something profound to come, he began to pontificate further about his views on homosexuality. I had heard enough, so I excused myself from the table. While I cannot fault my parents for standing by their convictions, I cannot condone their convictions. Because they're wrong. Nowhere does Jesus tell his disciples to "love thy neighbor" if the conditions are right.

The day after my daughter's confirmation service, when emotions rose like rushing waters through a narrow gate, I summoned my parents for a family discussion. I don't remember much of my lecture because anger can cloud one's memory. I reminded my parents that in all my years, I had never called into question their Republican politics. At that point in my political awakening, my objection to their support of Trump had absolutely nothing to do with politics and everything do with morality—"good people don't defend a bad man."[1] My dad agreed, because on the surface, it's a reasonable sentiment. But I think he missed my point entirely: Trump is a "bad man," ergo, how could a good person like you, Dad, support him? But perhaps my dad actually could agree with the statement because, in his mind, Trump isn't a bad man. Perhaps he feels Trump is a perfectly fine man to hold the most powerful seat in America. Or perhaps he knew that to admit anything else would question his own judgment. I don't know the reason, but without a doubt, the wrinkled confusion on my face must have triggered something in him. Like a deer in headlights, my dad eventually apologized for something I wasn't convinced he understood. In the end, he asked me what I wanted him to do, and I screamed, "Stop watching Fox News!"

1. Pavlovitz, "Good People," Jan 12, 2018.

Since The Floodgate, I'm pretty sure my family didn't appreciate my steadily increasing barrage of protest emails with articles attached like Tomahawk missiles targeting their support for Trump. At first those emails were about Trump's early actions, such as the Muslim ban and the "zero tolerance" policy at our southern border with Mexico. Then I tried a different tack. I introduced them to Heather Cox Richardson, a Harvard-educated American historian and professor at Boston College whose online following had ballooned since Trump's election. (Her daily newsletter, "Letters from an American," which began by recounting the events surrounding Trump's impeachment, was in 2020 the single most successful newsletter published by the Substack platform, with subscription revenues topping $1 million.) I hoped her clout and even-keel approach to placing current events within our historical framework would provide a neutral voice to the current debates. When this didn't work, I tried sending them articles by well-known and respected Republicans, Wheaton faculty members, and other reputable conservative news outlets. All of those efforts failed, too.

Sensing the continued strain and my feverish panic, my sister sent me a *Christianity Today* article entitled "What Psychology Offers Christians amid Political Polarization."[2] The main point of the article is that as Christians, we should practice "intellectual humility"—defined as an awareness that one's beliefs may be wrong—as a means of civil discourse because Jesus himself was humble. Let me be clear that I don't think for a second she sent this to me to point the finger, but I do feel it was her attempt to remind me to play nice. My response to her again went unanswered:

> My response to this article dated June 24, 2019, is that it's a little too late. Civility is thrown out the window when Christians continue to support our commander in chief who spews insults on decorated career military servicemen and women and current civil servants who oppose him. Civility is dead when Christians continue to support our president who perpetuates lies to the media and cries "fake news" when he feels threatened by negative publicity. Civility is abolished when Christians continue to uphold a president who seeks to abandon the rule of law and the very tenants of our Constitution, including checks and balances. Civility is lost when our president fast-tracks cabinet members who are not qualified for the job and fully vetted. Civility is dead when Christians knowingly voted for a man who unabashedly and unapologetically "grabs women by the pussy" and then boasts about

2. Zhou, "What Psychology Offers," June 24, 2019.

it. Civility is lost when Christians continue to support a president whose two years in office has seen a spike in hate crimes. Civility is lost when our commander in chief sides with known dictators then publicly disregards our own national intelligence.

None of the things I've mentioned above have anything to do the public policy or my problems with the GOP platform BUT with the lack of human decency we see in this presidency. He is not the right person for the job because he is not qualified. And I would argue there is no moral, civil, or religious justification for keeping Trump in the White House for another term in office. As American citizens and Christians (keeping with the audience of this article), we should all be appalled and irate because Trump is the exact antithesis of Christian values and, I would add, traditional Republican values.

So, the time for humility is long gone. The Bible is not just a blueprint for humility but also a call to action against injustice, poverty, and hate. And sometimes that response is not one of humility but civil action. Remember Jesus in the temple with the money changers—there was no humility there.

So, if you want to talk about hot button issues like foreign policy, gay marriage, abortion, I am honestly willing to try "intellectual humility" to the best of my ability. More listening and less talking. Humility to know that I don't have all the right answers and can learn from others with opposing views is something for me to strive. However, if the argument is why Trump is right for the presidency, there is no discussion because his vitriolic actions are too offensive and egregious.

The irony is that I have yet to see any "intellectual humility" from my family. While standing at her kitchen sink washing dishes, my sister told me Trump's win was "God-ordained" and "part of God's plan." I looked at her completely puzzled because I thought "the divine right of kings" was a concept from a very distant past. The American people have spoken, she countered, and their vote will help our "Christian nation."

"Christian nation?" I asked.

The United States of America was never intended to be a Christian nation since nowhere in our Constitution will you find the words church, Jesus Christ, God, or Christian. And didn't the pilgrims come to the New World *to escape* religious persecution? Not to mention that our Founding Fathers were secularists, insisting on the separation of church and state, and included in their number atheists, theists, and, for the most part, deists—those folks who rejected the miracles of the Bible and viewed God as the watchmaker who set the universe in motion and then stepped back to watch it spin. The "belief that the Founding Fathers were evangelical Christians is a fiction,"[3] and the idea that they built the Constitution based on the concerns of today's evangelicals is preposterous, if not downright comical. The phrase "under God" was added to our Pledge of Allegiance in 1954, and "in God we trust" was added to our currency in 1956. In fact, throughout the ages, from our first president George Washington, to Abraham Lincoln, Jimmy Carter, and even to Ronald Reagan, just to name a few, all specifically addressed the absolute belief in the separation of church and state. But that's not how my sister remembered her American history classes, she told me.

No, my family just doubles down, or earnestly says, "I'll have to get back to you," while never mentioning the subject again. Why are they unwilling to listen to other voices, even other Christian voices? Perhaps the fear lies in the notion that if they admit they were wrong to endorse Trump, the house of cards comes tumbling down, and with it their credibility. Humility is probably one of the hardest of Christian mandates because it strips us of the only power we feel we have left—our pride. While their unwavering support for Trump put undue weight on the branches of our family tree, it was the emotional toll of their silence that finally caused them to crack.

Of those fifty-five emails and articles I sent my parents following The Floodgate, my parents responded to precisely none. I don't know if they read them, or just hit the delete button. You'd think after sending the first half dozen I'd take the hint. I was confident, however, that one of those emails would hold the magic words to break the spell and allow them to see that Trump is the wrong person for the job. They'd been duped by a wolf in sheep's clothing. I'd just have to keep trying to find the right political cocktail to crack the code. In the end, I'm guessing they didn't appreciate their youngest daughter challenging them when, for most of her life, she ignored politics entirely. Who was I to come into the political arena in *medias res* and expect to be taken seriously? Especially as a screaming lunatic.

As a parent, I know that my kids will act out when they need something for which they don't have the words or understanding to articulate. When they were little, temper tantrums often erupted from hunger and fatigue, melt-downs from some injustice they were unable to name. My kids still joke about my favorite mantra to "use your words." But sometimes what my kids needed most was just to be held—no words—just the

3. Lang, "Christian Nationalism," line 107.

42

release of frustration in the protective arms of someone who loves them despite their behavior.

Sometimes adult children long for that same thing, to crawl back in time and into a parents' lap. My parents have identified my anger and witnessed my lashing out, but they have never asked me what it is really about—what's at the heart of my pain? What's the need the anger obscures? What's the thing under the thing? They never asked me to use my words to locate the root of my fear, and they've never offered any space to help figure this out together. Only silence. Why?

Almost a year later, I knew if we were to make any progress in reconciliation, I had to own my part of this mess:

> I owe you both an apology. A big one. I am very sorry for my anger toward you both. The anger in my voice and my harsh words have built a wall, and it's amazing, nothing short of grace actually, that you are still willing to talk with me—not just about politics, but about anything.
>
> The bonds of parent-child are strong, and I've always told my children there is nothing they could do that would change my love for them. I've learned that from you. Thank you for showing me that today and every day.
>
> Thank you also for loving me even when you wonder where the old Danielle has gone. This new "me" is not going away, and the old Danielle has never left. Maybe at almost fifty-one I'm finally coming into my own? But one thing that has never changed is my moral compass, and I attribute that to you, Mom. And I will thank my lucky stars every day that you gave me that fire. Now I've just got to figure out how to tame her. That's my work in progress.
>
> The only way this country is going to heal is if each [person] admits "I am part of this problem." And so, I am identifying my anger toward you and asking for your forgiveness.

My mom responded with an email that serves as the preface of this book. My dad's response follows below:

> Good morning favorite second daughter,
>
> Thanks for your recent loving email. I am a bit slow in completing a comprehensive reply that takes in a wide range of thoughts and emotions on my part. In the meantime, know that you are always completely loved. I wish I could give you a huge Dad hug. Maybe that would be enough said.
>
> Love ya, Dad

To this day my dad still hasn't articulated "a comprehensive reply," and I don't expect he ever will. Maybe he's biding time, holding out that this is just a phase for me, that I'll eventually come to my senses, or I'll just flat out give up and life will go back to the way it was. Or maybe he's biting his tongue fearing what he might say about liberals or Democrats or me. Or maybe he questions my intelligence, or my integrity. Or maybe I just lack political savvy and gravitas since coming into politics so late. Or maybe it's his pride. Or that he feels threatened. Or, as one family friend suggested, maybe he's avoiding this reckoning to save the relationship.

During a heated phone conversation, my sister asked me what I needed from my family for healing. "Accountability," I said. But for accountability to happen, there must be an honest look at one's contribution—good and bad—followed by a verbal acknowledgment. I always tell my children that an apology is only valid if you can name exactly what you are sorry for and strive to change your behavior so it doesn't happen again. The Christian equivalent to all of this is repentance. Admitting you are wrong or have wronged someone, coupled with sincere regret or remorse, then verbalizing that confession. Accountability is the whole package.

I named my sin toward my parents. But in that naming, I also was hopeful that my vulnerability might open the door for them to be honest as well, that they would look inward and identify their part in creating this mess. I was hoping my apology would serve as an invitation to join me in this state of openness, that they might be brave in admitting shortcomings, thus ultimately showing a shared commitment to our fragile relationship. My guess is they didn't take the invitation because they felt they didn't do anything wrong. There's no culpability for them because this has all been my doing (or undoing). I'm the one who has changed. But here's the catch. In spite of my hopefulness that they'd come around, and even in their unwillingness to admit even a smidgen of complicity, I knew for my apology to be true and earnest, it could only be offered without conditions or strings attached.

6

How Will Your Vote Reflect Jesus?

Don't tell someone you love them, and then vote for someone who will hurt them.

—@johnfugelsang

One of the ways I worked out the tension of an unraveling democracy during Trump's four years in office was by walking. That's what started this whole book-writing exercise. The thirty-minute round trip to the second lake gave me time to collect my thoughts and properly name my feelings. It's where I received the original inspiration to start a blog with my sister. It's where I remembered and connected lost memories. It's where I often would stop and jot ideas down on my phone. It was also the time I listened to podcasts that helped me understand our nation's history, past and present. Walking saved me.

One week before the election, my mother forwarded an email she received from the Episcopal Diocese of Pennsylvania. In the letter, Bishop Daniel Gutiérrez asks his congregants, "How will your vote reflect Jesus Christ?"—a rather unusual topic, I might add, coming from the church hierarchy. In the letter, the bishop pleads with his flock to vote, not through a party or candidate, but through faith, by asking, "How will your vote create a society that follows the greatest of all commandments: Love God and love your neighbor?"[1]

---

1. Gutiérrez, "How Will Your Vote," lines 21–23.

Without pointing fingers or naming names, he reminded folks of our then-current state of affairs under Trump, such as the normalization of violence and hate. He juxtaposed that with the promises we made in our baptismal covenant to "strive for justice and peace among all people, and respect the dignity of every human being."[2] Gutiérrez further implored fellow Christians to consider additional mandates when considering our candidates of choice. For example, do they promote peace, care for the poor, respect God's wondrous creation? The bishop provided corresponding scriptures to support each proclamation.

When I took Gutiérrez's challenge, I tried to think of ways Trump had sought to work for justice, peace, and respect of all people. But I couldn't get past Trump's 2018 order that separated children from their parents along our southern border with Mexico. When I protested to my family about this barbaric practice, my brother-in-law told me that it was Obama who built the cages that housed these children, and that maybe my anger was a bit misplaced. His comment stopped me in my tracks. Remember, I had not been paying attention to politics prior to 2016. After doing some of my own research, I learned that Obama had in fact built the enclosures as a temporary holding place until the parent(s) were properly processed through Immigration. Under Obama's watch, however, children were never separated from their parent(s) for more than a few hours, and none of them permanently. Obama neither used the cages as punishment for those seeking asylum, nor separation as a threat deterrent for future migrants attempting to enter the United States. Trump not only weaponized the cages, under his administration families were separated with little or no documentation that would facilitate future reunification of children with their parents. Trump essentially shoved them in cages then threw away the key. What kind of monster does that?

I thanked my mother for sharing the letter, and I was particularly moved by the bishop's reminder of our baptismal covenant. But I was curious: in light of her bishop's compelling letter, I asked Mom whether she still felt that Trump and his track record in office reflected Jesus Christ? Even though Biden is a practicing Catholic, my mother responded that "[she] cannot say either candidate reflects what we believe in our baptismal covenant . . . a strong faith is not a quality that politics invites."

I reminded her that that was not the point of the bishop's letter. "Your bishop is asking us to consider how 'our faith informs these decisions'

2. *Book of Common Prayer*, 417.

and then to vote accordingly," I wrote. She eventually sent me a two-page letter, which was a beautiful exegesis of her faith. In the end, however, she never answered the bishop's question.

My parents tend to avoid tough conversations. It's their *modus operandi*. I'm not sure whether it's a generational thing, growing up in an era when parents ruled and kids remained silent. Survival meant a stiff upper lip, to be seen and not heard. Almost every time I relayed a story about an incident at school or with peers, my mother's knee-jerk response was to ask the question, "How did you contribute to the problem?" As if I had a play in everything that happened in my life. Sometimes crappy things happen without provocation. Take my sophomore year in high school, for instance, when I had to beg my parents to meet with my English teacher, Ms. Gutwalt. Just as her name suggests,[3] she ruled her classroom, but with fear, seemingly finding pleasure in name-calling and demoralizing her students. I was so stressed in that environment, I couldn't learn.

My parents initially trusted the system, but they reluctantly humored my pleas and scheduled a meeting with Ms. Gutwalt. "How bad could it be," they asked? When my parents exited the classroom, they did so in silence, with wide eyes and mouths agape.

My dad's tour of duty in the Panama Canal Zone was one of the best experiences of my life. For starters, I was old enough to remember all of it. The expatriate life on a military base gave me the best of both worlds. I lived in a neighborhood and community filled with kids, and I got to explore the tropical rain forests and beaches of an exotic land. I water skied on Gatun Lake with cargo and cruise ships traveling through the Panama Canal in the distance. While hiking through the tropical rain forest with the Girl Scouts, I spotted a blue iridescent morning glory butterfly, black palms with their bark covered in three-inch spikes, and trails of leafcutter ants. I also saw the coveted and elusive quetzal bird with its scarlet breast, electric-blue-and-green tail feathers. I'll never forget the sound of the howler monkeys. Or the pollera dancers at the historic ruins. For a coming-of-age girl, they were magical days.

Because there were no Episcopal churches on base (at least none that I can recall), we traveled a short distance to the Episcopal Cathedral of St. Luke in downtown Panama City. I think my parents liked the idea of participating in a faith community off the military base. My sister and I both served as acolytes at St. Luke's, where I was baptized and confirmed

---

3. From the medieval German name Gottwald, meaning "God rule" or "good rule."

at the age of eleven. I'm proud that my confirmation and baptismal certificates are written in both Spanish and English. I loved the cathedral's old-world architecture with whitewashed walls and terra-cotta floors to keep us cool. The enormous windows with plantation shutters from floor to ceiling opened wide, allowing the breeze and an occasional bird to enter its sacred and historic space.

However, we didn't stay with this congregation for long. My sister, a teenager at the time, was desperate for a peer group and St. Luke's did not provide that. We had a makeshift Sunday School, but there simply weren't enough kids to gather for youth group in the evening. She began attending the nondenominational Crossroads Bible Church with some of her friends, and basically told my parents that she would no longer be attending St. Luke's. My parents resisted, but in the end decided to follow her into the non-denominational Bible church world. I imagine this migration provided a level of familiarity for my parents and comfort from the sound of Baptist hymns—"Trust and Obey," "The Old Rugged Cross," "What a Friend We Have in Jesus," to name just a few. Our family unit dove into the Crossroads community with both feet by attending Sunday morning worship and Sunday School followed by Sunday evening services, Wednesday night youth group and Bible study, and summer camps at the beach. Life revolved around church. And it was there that I met Heidi Oliver.

Heidi, my best friend in middle school, was a Cuna Indian from an indigenous tribe of the San Blas Islands, an archipelago off the coast of Panama, who had been adopted by White American expatriates. Malnourished as an infant, Heidi was much smaller in stature than even most people of her tribe, and her teeth suffered the consequences of a poor diet when she was an infant. Heidi was my friend and I couldn't have cared less how she looked.

My dad participated in an evening men's Bible study hosted by Heidi's parents. It was kind of like a house church extension of Crossroads, but just for men. Still, kids often tagged along and we socialized separately from the adults, eating pizza and watching movies. I looked forward to the men's Bible study every week. I also hung out at Heidi's on weekends because her house was the cool house with soda in the fridge and a trampoline in the backyard. One Saturday during the dry season, we decided to ride bikes through her neighborhood. Mrs. Oliver, standing in the kitchen near the garage door, vehemently objected that that wasn't a good idea. Puzzled, we both protested that we'd ridden bikes many times, and besides, it was still daylight. Her anger sprang from a place I'd never seen before, and she insisted riding bikes through the neighborhood was no longer safe, and then out of nowhere, screamed at us that it was *all my fault*. Every ounce of her rage was focused on me. I stood motionless, in shock.

At first, I didn't understand what I was being accused of. Her targeted rage at me, a child, spiraled into what I can only describe as an out-of-body experience. With tears welling in my eyes, I mechanically lifted the kitchen receiver off the wall hook and shakingly rounded the numbers on the rotary dial. With the phone cord coiled on the floor, I had enough extension to reach the privacy of an adjacent room where I begged my parents to come pick me up immediately. When they collected me, I was silent most of the car ride home because, in my young mind, I was trying to make sense of why Mrs. Oliver was so angry at me and what I could have done to contribute to her rage. Was it, whatever "it" was, actually my fault?

My mother, father, and I sat in the car as I relayed the events of the day through sobs, feeling the weight of being accused of something I didn't fully understand. I confessed that the only thing I could attribute her accusation to was something that happened to Heidi but that was completely unrelated to me. A few weeks earlier, when we were driving Heidi home after youth group, she confided in me that, months before, she had been raped. She didn't give me details, and frankly, I didn't really want to know. While I was interested in boys, sex was the farthest thing from my mind. Having sex forced upon you, unimaginable. I asked Heidi if she had gone to the police. She said no. I told her she had to tell her parents or someone who could help her. If she didn't, I would, because I thought that's what friends were supposed to do.

Heidi eventually told her parents, but the crazy thing is, to this day, I don't know how the situation resolved. Did she get medical attention like a rape kit? Was the perpetrator found? Was there even a perpetrator, or was it a lie made up for attention? Did Heidi have some undiagnosed mental illness? Was she telling the truth? The whole ordeal was shrouded in secrecy, and a big, empty mystery takes up space in my memories to this day. Had I been somehow to blame?

I quickly lost track of Heidi. I don't remember playing with her much after the incident, and I surely never wanted to return to her house. Moreover, how could I face the Olivers at church knowing they blamed me in some fashion for the heinous act perpetrated against their daughter? I begged my parents to intervene, to help sort out what happened in the Oliver's kitchen that fateful day. My parents grew silent, probably bearing the weight of having to confront dear friends about an uncomfortable situation. I knew their hesitancy meant they didn't want to jeopardize their friendship by making waves in the church. They didn't want to offend. Or maybe they questioned the validity of my story—did I really get the course of events right, or was I overreacting like a young girl might?

If either one of my children were accused of abetting a crime, you better believe I'd be on your doorstep wanting to hear your side of the story. But for my parents, it was my persistence, *not their conviction*, that was the catalyst for their eventual action on my behalf. The crazy thing is, Mrs. Oliver's apology was half-baked, and even I knew it. She never named what she was apologizing for, never said the words "I'm sorry" or "please forgive me," and called the whole ordeal a "big misunderstanding." While it didn't feel entirely right, I was not the adult in the room, but I hugged her anyway. And yet, a part of me walked away with lingering guilt, still unsure whether I was somehow to blame.

In our family, the one member who doesn't shy away from tough conversations is my brother-in-law, Tim. While he and I rarely agree on politics, he did reliably respond to many of my emails and articles even when I didn't hear from the rest of the family. He also took the time to send me articles that might challenge my argument or way of seeing things. And he wasn't afraid to spar with me and play devil's advocate. When I voiced my outrage about the crisis at the border, Tim was the only person to respond.

My own flesh and blood remained silent to this email thread about immigration at our southern border, perhaps because Tim was willing to take one for the team. I don't know. For Republicans, who espouse the sanctity of the traditional family, I found their silence and his response eye-opening and even more troubling. Not once in his argument did he mention the horrors of nursing babies being taken from their mothers. He showed no outrage about children crying themselves to sleep on the floor while wrapped in aluminum foil blankets. It's as if he lost track of the human side of this problem. Zero empathy. Politics disguised as justice swallowed the heart, soul, and overall well-being of a living, breathing, human being, even when these caged kids looked just like his own. Tim wrote:

> I'm very tired of people from both sides blaming Trump for this. Basic civics tells us that the executive branch enforces laws that are created by the legislative branch. Change will happen when the people demand Congress change the law. Let's do that and stop blaming the president for doing what he was elected to do.

With Republicans controlling both houses, Trump had every opportunity to change the laws. Instead, unlike any other president before him, Trump chose to use the full extent of the current laws to jail undocumented immigrants and *de facto* separate children from their parents as a weapon. Obama deported more immigrants than any sitting president, yes, but he did so without the long-term (and in many cases permanent) separation of families. Trump chose the least humane method, emotionally scarring thousands of children, hundreds who remain detained by the U.S. government and separated from their parents to this day.

It became increasingly clear that Trump had no interest in the sanctity of family. He basically used his immigration policy as a bargaining chip to get what he wanted: a border wall with a price tag of $25 billion of our tax dollars. Unsurprisingly, the only immigration bill he appeared willing to sign that would stop the separation also included his wall, a campaign promise made to his xenophobic, racist base. Yet more proof he was using innocent children as political pawns to promote his agenda, and that is simply inexcusable, abhorrent, and immoral. I didn't mince words:

> If you feel that Trump's interpretation of the law (jailing illegal immigrants) justifies separating families (not a law) is considered "doing what he was elected to do," then I'm afraid we are at an impasse.
>
> Blame rests with the president on this one, Tim. Any leader who would use children to gain his political agenda is evil. Plain and simple. And giving Trump a pass on this one is like Pilate washing his hands of Jesus' blood. I can't image ANY circumstance, not one, in which separating families is the RIGHT thing to do, the moral thing to do, or the American thing to do. We are better than this, as Americans and, more importantly, Christ-followers.
>
> Trump can stop this TODAY. And if all of us scream from the mountain top, then maybe he will change his policy.

Still, not one member of my family made a sound. I think they actually were quite happy with what Trump was doing—at last, a U.S. president who was willing to do that unmentionable thing under the guise of following the law without any consideration of long-term ramifications or weighing the results of crimes against humanity—especially the "least of these."

I really don't care, do u?[4]

---

4. The slogan on the back of Melania Trump's jacket as she boarded Air Force One on June 2018 to visit the children in cages at our southern border.

7

The Color of White

> never
> trust anyone
> who says
> they do not see color.
> this means
> to them,
> you are invisible.
>
> —Nayyirah Waheed @BlackLiturgies

> Being white means never having to think about it.
>
> —James Baldwin

I n addition to reading books, I participated in a couple of online challenges to help me understand my racism, biases, and White privilege.
One of the daily assignments was a link to "21 Racial Microaggressions You
Hear on a Daily Basis," a photography project where youth hold signs quot-
ing racial slurs that had been said to them. In one of the graphics, a Black
girl wearing big loopy earrings and a gorgeous smile holds a sign that says,
"You're really pretty for a dark skin girl." In another, a girl with olive skin
and wavy black hair holds a sign that reads, "You don't speak Spanish?"[1] I'm
pretty confident I've said some variation of these things over the course of
my life, completely ignorant of what exactly was coming out of my mouth. I

---

1. Nigatu, "21 Racial Microaggressions," frames 18, 7.

had never heard of the word "microaggression," so I looked it up, then sent the article to my sister because it made me think of her kids.

Unable to have biological children, my sister and brother-in-law adopted three beautiful biracial babies. The day my eldest nephew joined the family was such a happy day because it made my sister a mother, thus ending her long, lonely journey of infertility. None of us knew how to help her, but once this round, perfect, olive-skinned baby entered our lives, her devastation turned to utter devotion. We rallied around each new addition to their family, and out of abundant pride, we often joked that our family portrait looked like the United Nations because all three of their adopted children represented a different ethnicity. To this day, I remind my eldest nephew, even though he is an adult and married, I got the privilege of caring for him the first few nights as the newest member of our family. The law required a waiting period for out-of-state adoptions, so that put me, his new auntie, in charge.

My sister's response to the microaggressions article was twofold. First, her teenage kids had in fact experienced more than half of the microaggressions listed, and not simply as people of color but also as adopted children. Her response, one I did not see coming, generated a whole host of questions: Why am I just learning about this now? How is it possible that we never talked about their experiences with racism? Or heard from their lips about being racially profiled? Why on earth didn't my sister call a Come-to-Jesus family meeting so we could all learn from and rally around these kids? Why didn't we fight like hell on their behalf?

Why didn't I ask?

- Because I never saw my niece and nephews as anything other than full-fledged members of our White family.
- Because our Christian family's response historically has been not to make waves, instead to diffuse, soften, and pray.
- Because if we wait long enough, the problem might solve itself or go away.
- Because it wasn't *that* bad.
- Because if we don't name it, it isn't real.
- Because this is *their* private matter.
- Because admitting there is a racial problem automatically concedes they are different from us.
- Because we don't distinguish skin color.

When I was six months old, at the tail end of the Vietnam War in 1970, my family moved to Bangkok, Thailand. My young mother, who only had ever traveled between Boston, New York City, and her home in Quaker Hill, Connecticut, was thrust quickly and with no preparation into a new culture of a foreign land halfway around the world. Yet by the end of that four-year military tour of duty, my mother had learned how to bargain at the market with ease by swooping in behind the old women and demanding the same quality at the same price. She learned how the art of haggling involved walking away if the price wasn't right. She also learned to scuba in some of the world's most desirable diving locations and raced in regattas with my dad at the yacht club. Expatriate life in 1970s Bangkok was idyllic. For the family of a lowly army captain, we were living the high life: we had cooks and gardeners and house keepers and my beloved Som, our nanny. In fact, my mother had no desire to return to the States, but my father's commanding officer denied his petition for an extended tour, saying that with one more extension, he was afraid we'd never return. I think that was probably the point.

Bangkok was the only home I knew, and Som was my family. During the week, she lived in the maids' quarters behind our house. When mom was tired, Som would scoop me up. When my parents went on diving trips, Som begged them to leave me behind in order to protect me against the ravages of sun and heat, and they often acquiesced. There are old photographs of Som chasing me around the yard holding a bowl of fried rice or noodles to get me to eat one more bite. She bathed me in the huge barrels that collected rainwater, and cooled my skin from the heat with baking soda paste.

The natural results of growing up in a foreign country is I grew up bilingual. The funny thing is my father, who acquired proficient Thai language skills to communicate with his lab technicians, would speak to me in Thai, but I responded to him in English. At four years old, I understood the difference between race through language. Even though I couldn't comprehend the nuances of race, I understood there was a difference between Som and my dad. My dad was White, so I spoke to him only in English, but with Som, however, I spoke exclusively in Thai. Yet for me in my still-egocentric world, I rationalized that because I could speak Thai, I too must be Thai. With blond ringlets, I had an uphill battle convincing others of such.

As an adult, I certainly didn't see blackness or otherness in the pigment of my niece and nephews' skin. Aside from learning how to manage my niece's hair with oil relaxers, my sister didn't articulate any racial issues the kids might have faced. At least not to me. I think that was intentional wish-fulfillment so that we could assimilate as one happy homogeneous extended family unit. My mother proudly confessed to me not seeing their skin color because all she wanted to do was "love these babies." Instead of celebrating our differences, in essence, we ignored them in an ironic attempt for wholeness and unity. Yet this unbalanced equation meant my niece and nephews learned to live "White" while the rest of us couldn't be bothered even to notice what daily struggles they might have faced as people of color.

I was seven years old when *Roots*, the award-winning miniseries about slavery in the United States, aired on national television. It was the same era as my father's graduate school days with conservative talk radio. Without hesitation, my parents let my sister and me watch *Roots* as long as we were bathed and in our pajamas before the start of each episode. While I was sent to bed before the show ended each night, I followed the story with undaunted focus. I remember being deeply saddened and troubled by what happened to the African men and women who had been stolen from their homes, kidnapped, survived the inhumanity of the Middle Passage, to be enslaved and treated as subhuman in America. But once the series was over, it was back to watching *Mutual of Omaha's Wild Kingdom* and *Three's Company*. While *Roots* provided a perfect segue for having hard conversations about slavery and racism with me and my sister, my parents didn't seize the opportunity to talk to us about what we had just witnessed. It's as if this historical piece had no connection to our modern lives. Perhaps we didn't talk about such issues as a family because my parents didn't even see any connection between the history of enslaved people and our 1970s White American reality.

I think of the years lost in not seeing my niece and nephew's racial identities, which tangentially would have forced me to confront my Whiteness. I've since tried to put myself in their shoes, to feel what it means to be misunderstood and misjudged. The closest thing I can recount is my mother used to dress me in hand-me-downs from Jay Robbins, the neighbor boy across the street. With my short brown bowl cut and uneven bangs, thanks largely to my mother's fetish with hair scissors, I was often mistaken for a boy. The mispronunciation of my name didn't help either. Nor the fact that when I opened my mouth, my voice sounded like Barry White, or as Papa liked to call me, "the eighty-year-old midget." By kindergarten, I had developed acute laryngitis. Extensive voice therapy to remove the vocal folds impeding my speech involved training myself to speak at a lower octave. A star chart on the fridge rewarded me when I went a day without yelling, whispering, or singing. For a little girl who loved dresses and playing with dolls, there was nothing more horrifying than being misidentified as someone I was not—a boy.

Then there was the time when I was in kindergarten and my mom put me on the bus for a week-long day camp. All the kids were divided into groups by name tags in the shape of different flowers—sunflowers, daisies, roses, etc. It was bad enough that my best friend wasn't there on the first day to vouch for me. Apparently, they ran out of name tags, so my mother cut out a tulip from construction paper, wrote my name in big block letters, and pinned it to my shirt with the biggest safety pin imaginable. Kids pointed and giggled. Even the camp counselors didn't know what to do with me. I felt lonely and frighted because I didn't know where I belonged. But clothing and name tags are things that are easily changed. According to Debby Irving, author of *Waking Up White, and Finding Myself in the Story of Race*, color-blindness "actually maintains the very cycle of silence, ignorance, and denial that needs to be broken for racism to be dismantled."[2] By deduction, then, my silence, ignorance, and denial all make me complicit in furthering the racism my sister's children endured. And I did nothing.

And yet, we were able to see color in others. When I was a high school student, I remember relaying a story to my dad about something I witnessed at the end of algebra class. I overheard two Black girls sitting in front of me talking about a friend of mine. He had asked a White girl to the prom, but her parents wouldn't let her go with a Black boy. I told my dad how ridiculous this objection was, and that if my friend had asked me, I would have gladly gone with him to the dance. While skin color was the issue, I just saw a friend who wanted to go to the prom with a girl who happened to be White. No big deal. My father told me otherwise. At the time my dad questioned mixed marriages since the product of such unions is a biracial child who is neither fully Black nor White, and what a "cruel legacy" to give a child in this world. "It was only a dance, and not a trip down the aisle," I responded.

It was years later that I realized my own privilege in this story. Me, a White girl, had inserted myself into a private conversation between two Black girls without any invitation to do so. My logic dictated that because I, too, knew the boy of whom they were speaking, I was entitled to an

2. Irving, *Waking Up White*, 102.

opinion. Our common Black friend was the key to my access. Instead, they turned to me and without any words, shut me down instantly. I was mortified and embarrassed, and knew I crossed an invisible line. I was not a part of their world, and they sure as hell weren't inviting me in just because I felt entitled to it. I slithered down in my seat, when I wish now, I would have had the understanding to apologize.

The second half of my sister's response to the article about microaggressions was just as revealing, but for totally different reasons. She begins her dissent of the term "microaggression" with a little phrase that is easily overlooked: *from my experience*. Isn't this precisely the problem we White people share? By interjecting our White experience into a Black person's experience of microaggression, we attempt to nullify, or at the very least, offer an alternate interpretation that makes us feel better and look less like jerks. That microaggression isn't what it seems, my sister continues, because it's actually "ignorance—not knowing combined with curiosity."

I completely understand how curiosity can muddle the water. I was at my daughter's lacrosse practice years ago, and started small talk with another mother I had never met before. I did not know who her daughter was, so the women pointed in her daughter's direction and told me her jersey number. She was the tall, athletic Black girl running circles around the other girls on the team. In my haste to understand the connection of this White mother with a Black daughter, I asked, "Is she yours?" then quickly realized I misspoke when another woman's side-eye piercingly asked *did you really just say that out loud*? What I really meant to ask—"Is she adopted?"—was not much better, however. Completely flummoxed, I finally just apologized and said that her daughter was beautiful and looked just like my adopted niece. At that time, I didn't know there was an official sociopolitical term for what I said. Nor did I understand that what just exited my mouth was a fine example of a microaggression toward a White mother and her biracial daughter. In spite of my ignorance, the woman was more than gracious, most likely because she's heard similar microaggressions since the day she brought her daughter into the world. But looking back now, the bigger question is, how was any of this my business? And moreover, why did I feel this was important information for me to know?

The term microaggression is really a compound word made from two very simple words (small + hostile), yet the result is a harsh-sounding word with layers of meaning. I get that my sister feels the very word sounds harsh and divisive. It is. It's only divisive to the White person being called out for the offense because the Black, Indigenous, Hispanic, Asian, or LGBTQ+ persons on the receiving end have carried the brunt of that divisiveness for centuries. My sister continued, "I think microaggressions assumes the angry/violent side for all comments. Perhaps calling it microaggression is a piece that furthers the divide, . . . it appeared to me as a *microignorance*."

And there it is—soften the blow to our White egos by creating a kinder, gentler word that gives White people yet another escape route from accountability. Irving points out that the word "ignorance, which implies a passive state of being, shares the same root with the word 'ignore,' which implies an active choice."[3] Just because we White people refuse to learn about racism, all of its ugly truths, and the many ways we perpetuate it, doesn't give us the right to play the ignorance card when it suits us. Our ignorance is not a pass, and neither is it the responsibility of those in the minority to educate those of us in the majority. We don't get to have it both ways.

What became evident during this heated exchange is that my sister either didn't understand the definition of microaggression or just chose selective parts. Microaggressions, a term originally coined in 1969 by the African American Harvard professor and psychiatrist Dr. Chester M. Pierce, are "brief and commonplace daily verbal, behavioral, or environmental indignities, whether intentional or unintentional, that communicate hostile, derogatory, or negative racial slights and insults toward people of color."[4] Whether it was my sister's intention or not, her "microignorance" seemed more concerned with protecting the ignorant one/oppressor, rather than the minority person who has been wronged.

To reinforce her point about "microignorace" being the better term, my sister shared another experience, this time involving a Korean friend. While shopping together in a convenience store, her Korean friend had a minor exchange with a White store clerk about an item she lost in the store. The miscommunication occurred because the clerk could not understand her thick Korean accent, and consequently, she made an unkind statement about it. My sister's interpretation of the events is so indicative of what gets us White people in trouble—we make excuses for our people's bad behavior. My sister essentially defended the White clerk, telling me she didn't think she was being aggressive or "trying to put her friend down."

But my sister's entire explanation of this event stems from her own White perspective with "I didn't get the sense" and then "it appeared to

---

3. Irving, *Waking Up White*, 81.
4. Giegerich, "Right to Not Remain Silent," lines 10–12.

me." I wasn't there, so I don't know the full story; however, nowhere in my sister's story does she mention what her friend thought about what happened to her in the store. Why would my sister omit such an important element of the story?

What I'd like to ask my sister now is how exactly did *she* work "toward positive bridge building," in this instance? Did she ask her friend if she was okay? Did they talk through the disparaging things the clerk said and why the miscommunication happened in the first place? Did my sister march right back in the store and confront the clerk about how she offended her friend? Did my sister offer the clerk a more productive and less offensive response for the next time something like this might happened? Did they celebrate her friend's acquired English proficiency while the store clerk had zero appreciation of her second language skills? I don't know, but I surely hope so. Yes, attitude is a choice, and so is making excuses.

Words matter. My sister and I can at least agree on that. In her rebuttal to me she argues "since we both know how powerful words can be, we would all do well to consider what we call things so that they not only bear truth but lead to healing." *This is my point exactly.* Let's use words correctly, call a spade a spade, stop saying dumb-ass things to our BIPOC neighbors, teach people how to treat others by our own example, and heal this broken country. Let me put this another way. If I witness a microaggression, I'm not going to infuse my White privilege as part of the narrative or redefine the terms to accommodate my fragile ego so I can go on my merry way into ignorant bliss and call it a day—I'm going to bear truth by calling it a microaggression, and then I'm going to work damn hard to make sure it doesn't happen again.

To my sister's credit, she has since completed Diversity, Equality, and Inclusion (DEI) training as an extension of her professional growth. I'm really proud of her, and I commend her search and her quest for knowledge. I appreciate she sees the lack of diversity in her almost all White church—perhaps something she can help change for the better. But I'm also curious. Curious because even with her title of executive groups director, my sister will never be able to serve on her church's elder board, a group of decision-makers who help govern the church, because she's a woman. And if there are any gay couples in her church, will they be granted the full rights and privileges of holy matrimony? Or even a blessing? How does one practice full and complete inclusion when the interpretation of one's religion overtly flouts it?

My sister hasn't said much about her DEI training, so I took the opportunity to ask her about it during our last family trip. Normally, all twelve of us rent a beach house but that year, because schedules were so tight and we waited too late, we compromised on a shorter vacation at a lake. While the two of us sat atop the floating dock, I ask her if she had changed her mind about systemic racism.

Months earlier we had an animated conversation about systemic racism in the form of voter suppression, yet both my sister and brother-in-law couldn't get past "systemic" and "racism" in the same sentence. Yet again, another semantic stumbling block that hindered any movement toward bipartisanship. Frankly, I was stunned that we first had to unpack "systemic" before we could even get to the heart of the matter—voting rights. My sister questioned whether racism permeated all of our society's systems. But when I asked her why more Black babies die than White babies, why do Black people earn proportionately less than White people, or why do fewer Black families own homes than White families, she had no answer, but that she would get back to me.

My brother-in-law did have an answer, however. But he framed his argument differently: America is not a racist country because we've had a Black president and currently a Black vice president. He continued that because America voted for Black presidents proves we don't have racist systems in place. If we had, they never would have won, he said.

The funny thing about his argument is U.S. Senator Lindsay Graham, a Republican from South Carolina, had said exactly the same thing on national television. And when the U.S. Representative Ilan Omar, a Democrat from Minnesota, a Muslim and a woman of color, was asked about Graham's comments, her retort put it all in perspective: "It's as if saying we don't have poverty issues in this country because we have millionaires and billionaires."[5] Or here's another: anti-Semitism doesn't exist because my doctor, lawyer, and accountant are all Jewish. Obama and Harris were elected through record number of BIPOC citizens voting *in spite of* the myriad of systemic voter suppression laws—not because systemic voter suppression doesn't exist.

My sister's responded that yes, she had changed her views about systemic racism enough to admit that it does exist, however, "just not in all systems." Not wanting to jinx the progress, we left it at that. Weeks later, though, I followed up by asking her which systems are not racist. After

5. Crocket, "If Lindsey Graham Claims," lines 34–35.

first consulting with my brother-in-law, she suggested that major league sports aren't systemically racist because players are hired for their talent and not their skin color. Superficially, it may seem a reasonable response, especially since more Black athletes dominate sports such as professional football and basketball.

But that's the nature of racism. It's pernicious, lurking just under the surface, out of view. How is it that Kaepernick takes a knee and is still blackballed from playing in the NFL, yet no White athlete taking a knee in solidarity has ever been fired from the league? Or how is it that Aaron Rodgers, who refused the COVID vaccine and lied about his vaccination status, a potentially lethal decision compared to Kaepernick's sociopolitical gesture of protest, is merely slapped on the wrist? Or how is "race norming," the practice of using stereotypes about Black people's cognitive function to determine concussion settlement funds, only a side story? Why aren't there more NFL Black head coaches and executives when more than 70 percent of the NFL players are Black? Why are there no Black franchise owners in the NFL? And what, if anything, will come of Brian Flores' lawsuit against the NFL for its racist hiring practices?

If you don't see the color of someone's skin, then it's much easier to dismiss the existence of systemic racism. When the same rules don't apply to everybody, there is White privilege and there is racism. But you have to be willing to look for it, and then you have to call it by its name when you see it.

8

Instagram and My White Privilege

> Some people have a hard time recognizing privilege, saying "I work hard. I don't get things handed to me." I understand that. Here's how I respond: privilege isn't bonus points for you and your team. It's unfair penalties the other team gets that you don't.
>
> —Marie Beecham @mariejbeech

> It's a privilege to lose interest in dismantling racism.
>
> —@revolutionartshop

When I started this new journey of political and social awakening, I had been following only a small group of friends on Instagram. But once I began to see who they were following by reading their posts, I expanded my social media repertoire to include W. Kamau Bell, Dr. Bertice Berry, Black Liturgies, the ACLU, the Southern Poverty Law Center (SPLC), and last but not least, The Food Network. My feed today is a beautiful cornucopia of social justice mixed with tantalizing recipes and a healthy side of friends and family updates. Yes, I still spend too much time scrolling, but I'm also learning. Lots.

One of the things I've noticed through my scrolling is how colloquial language is used to bolster political agendas. This concept, based on the understanding that language is fluid and changes over time, is nothing new. But social media has propelled it into the fast lane of mainstream culture and into the hands of the young and the old alike. Even before smart phones, we saw this years ago when "global warming" slowly morphed into "climate change," and "anti-abortion" became "pro-life." Such subtle shifts in language can change our perspective, sometimes without us even noticing. And that's the whole point.

The addition of "woke," "cancel culture," and, most recently, "critical race theory" (CRT) to our digital and cultural vocabulary demonstrates such adaptation gaining momentum, and, consequently, a political war of words intensifying rapidly. Thanks to the Rev. Esau McCaulley, a Wheaton College (Illinois) professor and author of the book *Reading While Black*, I learned on his Instagram feed that "woke" is a term Black people used for years before it became part of mainstream parlance in the last few years. The term was first coined in the 1930s in a song by Lead Belly, who encouraged his listeners to "stay woke," to pay attention to racial injustices, especially when traveling in the South. Within the Black community, it later became a term of celebration. To describe someone as "woke" meant that they are a socially conscious person striving to bring about positive change. Yet because of right-wing media and its bellicose talking heads, McCaulley says the word woke "was gentrified, colonized, and turned toxic by people who never loved our [Black] community. That was a sin and we deserve an apology."[1]

Moreover, according to Danté Stewart, an award-winning writer, ordained minister, and author of *Shoutin' in the Fire: An American Epistle*, the most current iteration of a White person's usage of "woke" has taken a far more sinister connotation: "the word 'woke' is just another term for Black. When people are talking about 'wokeness,' they are talking about Black equality, Black dignity, and Black liberation. That's what they hate. They are anti-Black. It has always been about White supremacy and power."[2] The word "woke" often gets tossed around in my family of origin, but I wonder if those family members who use it would change their tune knowing they're perpetuating a gross perversion of the word that is now used to deride the very community who coined it and celebrates it.

The same is true with "cancel culture." I hadn't really paid much attention to it because, well, frankly I don't watch Fox News, whose anchors used "cancel culture" seven times more often than MSNBC.[3] But I knew the idea was blowing up in Republican circles because my sister asked me

1. McCaulley, "That was the meaning," Instagram, June 13, 2021.
2. Stewart, "Let's be clear," Instagram, January 20, 2023.
3. Bump, "Fox News Talks about 'Cancel Culture' and Political," lines 65–67.

not to "cancel" her whenever we disagree on politics. What does that even look like, I wondered? Like wokeness, cancel culture has a history prior to the political mainstream grabbing onto its coattails in recent years. While the term has a longer and varied past, "cancel culture" became part of our collective consciousness in 2017 with the #MeToo movement, when the offensive comments and abusive behaviors of Hollywood celebrities such as Bill Cosby, Harvey Weinstein, and R. Kelley were canceled before they ever stepped foot into a court of law.[4]

Like most things, how you define cancel culture comes down to which side of the fence you hang your lasso. A recent article from the Pew Research Center finds that nearly as many Republicans as Democrats are familiar with the term, so it's not out of a lack of hearing it. The key difference, however, is how it's defined. Their research suggests that more Republicans see cancel culture as a form of censorship or punishment, whereas, more Democrats see it as a matter of holding folks accountable for their actions.[5] This polarization might appear to be similar to the cartoon where two people, facing each other, are looking down at a large number written on the sidewalk. One person argues he sees the number 6, but the man directly across from him insists it's the number 9. In this example, are both individuals right, depending on their perspective? Does "cancel culture" always just boil down to a matter of perspective? I would argue, no.

The irony here is the same social conservatives who rage against "cancel culture" have mastered the tools of cancel culture to their advantage. For example, long before the term was really even a thing, the then Dixie Chicks (recently rebranded to The Chicks after George Floyd died at the hands of the police), were blacklisted in the country music industry at the height of their careers when they publicly criticized Republican president George W. Bush over the Iraq War in 2003.[6] They exercised their freedom of speech, so was the swift and harsh backlash from their fans and the music industry a matter of censorship or accountability?

In a more recent example, the Republican congresswoman Liz Cheney, who voted with Trump 93 percent of the time,[7] was sanctioned and completely ostracized by her own party when Speaker Nancy Pelosi, a Democrat, appointed her to the House Select Committee on the

4 Greenspan, "How 'Cancel Culture' Quickly Became," lines 11–13.

5. Vogles, "Americans and 'Cancel Culture,'" lines 74–75.

6. Blackwelder, "Dixie Chicks talk cancel culture," lines 7–9.

7. Brewster, "Who's More Loyal?," lines 18–20.

January 6 Attack. Consequently, she lost her seat at the midterms when her constituents voted her out of office. Censorship or accountability? In the end, Cheney's commitment to seek answers about January 6 for the American people unleashed unrelenting Republican censorship. Republicans defending Trump's Big Lie didn't take kindly to her holding their feet to the fire—so they did the very thing they publicly denounce in the war on culture—they cancelled her.

The Republican success in snowballing the overall effect of the "culture wars" is that they understand human nature. They are banking on the knowledge that most people won't do the research and everybody wants to be right. In revisiting cartoon analogy about the number on the sidewalk, if you're only concerned with perspective—your perspective—then yes, you can argue it's a 6 and not a 9 until you're blue in the face. But you could still be dead wrong. Until you stop and do the research—find the person who wrote the number and ask him, or step back to see if any other numbers come before or after it, or place the number in its context (on a door or a side of the building)—then you really can't be sure if it's a 6 or a 9. It's those people, the ones boasting that their uninformed opinions based on "alternative facts" are as equally valid as verifiable facts, whose actions fan the flames of the culture wars, thus accelerating the division in our country.[8]

If ever there were an opportunity to justify the value of social media as a learning tool, and not just a time-sucking waste, this would be it. By choosing to follow individual people and groups outside of my social circle, Instagram has given me a window into the Black community that I would not otherwise be privy to. For example, the misunderstanding of "White privilege," part of the lexicon of hot-button Republican misinformation propaganda, means virtually every BIPOC organization has produced some type of meme to help us White people get it. Many of these memes, while corralled by character limits, are masterfully crafted, loaded with provocative insights that make me stop and think in ways I never had.

One source of such social media learning comes from my morning devotions with Dr. Bertice Berry (@drberticeberry on Instagram), a Black American sociologist, author, lecturer, educator, and fellow Episcopalian. Her invitation to her followers includes: "Hi! I'm Dr. Bertice Berry, and I want to tell you a story." Not only does she cozy up into my personal space when her face fills my entire phone screen, but it's also her storytelling magic that is so up-front and life-changing. She is a stranger,

8. @progressivechristianity, "Just because you are right," Instagram, April 24, 2023.

yet she intimately draws close to us, so close you can see the veins in her eyes and sometimes the pool of tears before it streams down her cheek. Her experiences with racism and discrimination are often hard to hear, but her truth is so compelling because it's filled with grace and love that I can't help but stop, listen, and relearn.

Before my political awakening, I had always attributed "White privilege" to someone who had "more ____" (fill in the blank) than me—money, material goods, education, opportunities, connections—and was undeserving of it. A kid born with a silver spoon in her mouth. Nope, that's just plain privilege. But when you attach the "White" modifier, the meaning changes almost entirely. White privilege isn't about individual White people's success or struggle; it's about an uneven playing field for anybody else who isn't White.

That epiphany came from a meme I shared with my brother-in-law not long after the 2016 election. I understood my White privilege as the following: I didn't have to really pay attention to election cycles, changes in the law, or Supreme Court decisions because, for the most part, they didn't affect me personally. Regardless of our government's swing to the left or the right, I could still live my life entirely without incident, feeling free to move about the cabin, if you will. Never has my skin color kept me from doing anything I wanted to do, nor do I live in fear that someday that might change.

Simply put, as a White person, I can play video games in my home without fear of police shooting and killing me through my window. But Atatiana Jefferson could not. I can also walk home from the corner convenience store at night without fear of getting killed by police. But Elijah McClain could not. I don't have to worry about my son getting pulled over and killed for a minor traffic violation. Duante Wright's mother could not. That's White privilege. The thing is, *every* Caucasian American, rich or poor, has White privilege. Just like the gift of God's grace, White privilege is there whether we accept it or not. It's coiled in our DNA, exposed in our melanin, and ingrained in our thinking—but what we do with it marks our true character.

The first step for me in combating the effects of White privilege was by naming it in my own life. Thanks to Irving's book, I came across Peggy McIntosh, founder of the National SEED (Seeking Educational Equity and Diversity) Project. Her concept of White privilege is quite simple: White people carry with them at all times an invisible weightless backpack filled with special provisions such as maps, visas, tools, and blank checks. She then provides twenty-six everyday experiences that highlight ways White people benefit from their skin color. For example, it wasn't until 2022—one hundred years after Johnson & Johnson began selling BAND-AID brand adhesive bandages—did Black and Brown customers have the option to choose a "flesh-colored" bandage matching their skin tone. I hadn't considered that problem before *because I'd never had that problem*, thus further emphasizing that the century-old peach-colored bandage is the visual reminder of White-dominated medicine.[9] I never once considered how the "White" flesh-tone bandage on a Black person actually draws attention to the wound—the very opposite of what it was intended to do for White people. Checking off such examples of the privilege that I take for granted everyday became for me the catalyst for deeper searching.

While memes lit the match, my passion took flame when I participated in a three-part series through the Episcopal Diocese of North Carolina called "The Journey to Racial Equity." The Rev. Dr. William Barber II, his voice as fulsome and powerful as his stature, rolled out his Repairers of the Breach PowerPoint. But the voice that resonated with me the most came from a different guest speaker, a soft-spoken, middle-aged White woman named Debby Irving. Her book, *Waking Up White and Finding Myself in the Story of Race*, felt like she was speaking directly to me with her slippered feet propped up on my coffee table. In her book, Irving patiently explains the words we hear tossed around the airwaves—White privilege, systematic racism, class, and discrimination—in the context of her own upbringing. I wanted to savor every page, so I limited myself to no more than two chapters per sitting. Read. Reflect. Repeat. I instantly resonated with her because my story so closely mirrored hers.

I grew up listening to AM talk radio; its angry commentary filled my head like second-hand smoke. For years my dad listened to conservative radio and later to Rush Limbaugh, the same conservative broadcaster who was awarded the Presidential Medal of Freedom by Trump at the State of the Union address in 2020. On the flip side, Dad also listened to NPR's Nina Totenberg and *All Things Considered*. My personal favorite were the funny, folksy, and informative car enthusiast hosts of *Car Talk*, Tom and Ray Magliozzi, aka "Click and Clack the Tappett Brothers," native of Cambridge, Massachusetts, and both graduates of MIT. As a PhD candidate at the University of Texas in Houston, my dad picked up various pastimes as a way to decompress from his heavy research and writing. When I was in elementary school, his odd work hours and decompression routines meant some days I'd come home in the afternoon to his freshly

9. Gupta, "Redefining 'Flesh-Colored' Bandages," lines 10–14.

baked cottage cheese dill bread. Running and training for marathons also provided stress release. Instead of buying a new pair of shoes, however, his grad-school budget warranted frugality. While the rant-filled rhetoric from radio talking heads reverberated off the garage walls, my dad meticulously smoothed hot glue to his worn-down soles.

Irving's book invited me to reflect deeply about my past by providing guided questions at the end of each chapter. For example, in chapter 8, "Racial Categories," Irving discusses how she learned that "race is more of a social construct than a biological certainty."[10] She, like most of us, carried with her false assumptions about each race having their own differing abilities. For example, she assumed all Black people have rhythm, as evident in jazz music, and an astounding athleticism, because of players like Michael Jordan. She asks the reader if we've given much thought to whether or not skin color signifies inherent difference, followed by every good teacher's discussion tool of "Why or why not?" It was through these chapters and provocative questions that I wrestled with the differences within my family. Our politics and theology are vastly different, so where is the common ground? One of the topics about which I felt we might have shared views is the problem of racism in our country. What was I thinking?

For several months my family and I read articles and shared video clips about racism, Black Lives Matter, protesting, and other social justice issues in the attempt to learn from various perspectives. We collectively agree racism is a stain on American history, but in my naïveté, I assumed we would also be able to name it when we see it. Then came January 6, 2021.

I could not believe what was happening on television. How could such an egregious attack on our democracy occur simultaneously with such meager defense? And where in the hell were the police, the National Guard, or the State Troopers? For God's sake, somebody *do* something! We are the United State of America, and citizens holding American flags don't assault police, in broad daylight no less. What the hell is happening? And then it dawned on me, where is the president? He could stop this. In my panic, I did the same thing I did when the second tower fell on 9/11, I called my family. My sister was about to head into a meeting at work and said she'd watch it later. I was annoyed and felt she didn't grasp the severity of the situation. I got my parents' voicemail, but my dad later texted me that he was following on the radio while traveling in the car. He, too, was shocked.

10. Irving, *Waking Up White*, 38.

Wrapped with fear, two days later I sent the following email to my sister and parents:

> I can only hope you are as incensed as I am that radicalized American terrorists stormed, looted, shed blood, and desecrated our nation's Capital, the symbolic seat of American democracy. I'm flat-out scared because look how close this insurrection came to toppling our government. If this were ever to happen again with a more cunning president, a few corrupt judges, elected officials, and police officers, could they succeed? Could constitutional checks and balances withstand their corruption? Time will tell. However, if it was attempted on January 6, 2021, my guess is it could more easily happen again.
>
> And perhaps, like me, you might also be asking yourself how we got to this point.
>
> Each one of us has some response, I know, to that question. Deep-seeded tropes bubble up. Old ideas we've worn like badges of honor resurface from our memories. Pride rears its ugly head. I say it's time for all of us to fully lift the veil and address this head-on, fully transparent, warts and all. Change starts with me and you.
>
> We started this exercise last summer, but in my opinion, failed. Instead, we increased the divide between us as we each retreated to our corners of avoidance, Christian security, denial, self-righteousness, and anger. And then came the election.
>
> It dawned on me a few weeks ago that our dysfunction around politics is akin to that of a reading club. We are all committed to reading, but when we all sit down finally to discuss the book, we can't because we each read a different book. How can we discuss the chapters when we each read from a different source?
>
> I propose we try something new.
>
> I actually hope we can start our own family discussion around what we read together—this time, from the same book.

I sent them each a copy of *Caste: The Origins of Our Discontents*, by the Pulitzer Prize-winning bestselling author Isabel Wilkerson. The book is a deep dive into the intersection of Hitler's dehumanizing practices, India's caste system, and America's historical racism and White supremacy. My parents and sister thanked me for the book, began reading it, but we haven't discussed it together, even once. My mom did say she could barely get through the introduction but she would try to read a few pages each day. I don't know why I would have assumed they would read it, especially if they don't even believe systemic racism exits in every facet of American life. The only books my sister has given me as gifts over the years or suggested I read in today's political climate were written by conservative Christians. I rationalize that she does this for two reasons: either she is attempting to counter my usually liberal arguments or she hopes to redirect my path down the straight and narrow. Probably a little bit of both.

My mother pooh-poohs racial social justice theory like its somehow antithetical to Scripture. I can tell because she rolls her eyes or shifts her posture whenever the phrase enters our conversation. When I pressed her on it, she sent me an email recommending a video called "Uncle Tom: An Oral History of the American Black Conservative." She encouraged the family to watch it because it provides "another point of view that supports [her] understanding of building and encouraging American people." My sister followed up with a text confirming her approval. The executive producer was Larry Elder, whom my mother described as an "elder statesman." At that time, I'd never heard of him, so I started doing some research.

Larry Elder is a Black attorney, bestselling author, and nationally syndicated conservative radio talk show host. A graduate of Brown University, most recently, Elder ran for governor of California in an attempt to unseat Democrat Gavin Newsom in a recall election, losing by a wide margin. He is a contrarian, prides himself as the "sage from South Central," and to some is even farther to the right than Trump himself. He opposes gun control, minimum wage, and doesn't believe a gender wage gap exists. He even said recently that former White slave owners are owed reparations.[11] Yes, you read that right. White slave owners are owed for compensation lost when their "property" was taken from them after the Civil War. Elder, who a *Los Angeles Times* columnist dubbed the "Black face of white supremacy,"[12] hobnobs with other Black conservative provocateurs such as Candace Owens, a media personality and anti-vaxxer who notoriously touted COVID-19 conspiracy theories across her platforms throughout the global pandemic.

Elder is also a regular contributor to the *Epoch Times*, a conservative news source with the tag line "Truth and Tradition." My parents subscribe to the *Epoch Times*, and while thumbing through it, I noticed none of the headlines reflected the most urgent conversations of the day. There was nothing about COVID on the front page or anything about it below the fold. Curiously, instead the cover only mentioned China. *Anti*-China, that is. After some further research, I discovered that the *Epoch Times* was founded

11. Keith, "California Recall Candidate Larry Elder," lines 1–4.
12. Smith, "Column: Larry Elder."

by John Tang, a member of the cult called Falun Gong, who, among other things, undervalues science and medicine for human advancement. It's not surprising then that the newspaper lacked anything significant or helpful about the pandemic for its subscribers; in fact, the *Epoch Times* misled its readership by "disseminating false or misleading information about CO-VID-19, or the supposed dangers of vaccines."[13] While originally an obscure publication handed out freely on streetcorners, once the company tapped into the powers of promotion at Facebook, it catapulted itself into the global market and landed right in my parents' living room.

It's also the same "newspaper" my mother claimed was her source when she pronounced that BLM and Antifa were to blame for the January 6 riots at the Capitol. I told her that this information was undeniably false, with zero proof from any reputable news source to back it up. And all she had to do was look at the video clips playing round the clock on every news channel (except Fox). Besides, weren't the hordes of White people waving Trump flags and wearing full-MAGA military gear a dead giveaway about who was behind this revolt? And what about those Christian flags that dotted their battlefield? Did my parents see those, too?

This dystopian conversation got me thinking about the newspaper's tagline of "Truth and Tradition." I had to let that simmer for a minute. Tradition in what sense of the word? In the sense of ideas, customs, or beliefs handed down from generation to generation? What if that tradition is a false narrative, or at the very least, an incomplete one? Is it still "truth" and worthy to be passed down to our children and their children? I can't think of a more out of touch objective for a media source, that is, unless you really do want to keep things exactly the way they've always been done. Change, after all, is often revolutionary.

Even the most cursory Google searches shows that Elder is not part of any mainstream media, and I'm guessing that's one reason why my family gravitates toward him. I watched a few of his YouTube videos slandering Democrats, of which I am one, with his no-nonsense approach to politics. He's a fast talker who doesn't give you time to process one claim before he's on to the next, and by the end your head hurts and your heart is racing. He is also a master of self-promotion, touting his books and videos. But I can see why my family listens to him. He is a finely educated, lavishly employed, impeccably dressed, eloquent Black man who exudes self-confidence on camera. He is also the same person donning a fluffy white bathrobe (an

13. Loucaides and Perrone, "Media Giant," lines 22–23.

interesting color choice, I might add) while calling Presidents Barack Obama and Joe Biden "race-card hustlers" and promoting #WeveGotACountryTo-Save and #SystemicRacismIsACon on Instagram.[14]

How, exactly, is my mother's suggested "Uncle Tom" video supposed to help our conversation about racism? I wonder why many Christians, my family included, listen to voices like his. What does Elder offer that validates their feelings about race and racism? By all standards, Elder is a success story—he climbed the corporate ladder through hard work and by navigating the system, perhaps with a boost from affirmative action—and made it to the top. What, then, does he seek to gain by unabashedly promoting the idea that systemic racism, *aimed at his own people*, is nothing but a farce?

I guess my family has found their token Black spokesperson whose own words upend the need for systemic change in our country. Because of Elder's voice and others like him, the White community and my family who listen to them must feel a tremendous sense of relief. If Elders, a Black man, believes systemic racism is a fake construct, then we White people have absolutely nothing to worry about. We are not culpable for any wrongdoing toward the POC communities from our past or in our present; we're free to move forward with the mindset of "business as usual." Truth and Tradition. Who am I to argue?

> While truth does not always rest with the majority—neither does it reflexively reside with the outliers, the exceptions, the anomalies:
>
> 1. The black Trump supporter that "tells it like it is" and makes you feel better about your racist politics.
>
> 2. The doctor on the periphery who confirms what you want to hear about a hidden cure.
>
> 3. The isolated scientist who "exposes" climate change and makes you comfortable with the exploitation of our environment.
>
> If you seek truth only in the margins, it's likely not truth that you are pursuing—but rather a mirror for your own biases and pre-conceptions. Some will follow truth wherever it leads, no matter how uncomfortable; others will lead themselves to comfort—and pretend they've found truth.[15]

14. Elder, Instagram video, August 6, 2021.

15. @thesubversivelens, "While truth does not always rest with the majority," Instagram, July 31, 2020.

9

The Canadian and Fake News

> History that exalts a nation's strengths without ever examining its shortcomings, that prefers feeling good rather than thinking hard, that seeks simplistic celebration over a full understanding—well, that's not history; that's propaganda.
>
> —@KevinMKruse

I'm pretty sure my father sent me the following two emails by mistake. The first, with a subject line "A Canadian's view of Donald Trump," he also sent to my sister, his two brothers, and dear family friends who are my godparents. The only political email coming from my parents naturally piqued my interest, so of course I read it. Multiple times. Much to my horror, it was, for lack of a better term, propaganda to puff up the believers, to embolden the Right by slandering and demeaning the Left with flat out lies, half-truths, and loads of self-righteous indignation. The second email, reinforcing the sentiments of the first, was an all-White male band singing "Proud to Be an American," complete with cowboy hats, big buckles, and waving American flags.

Like many spammy or ridiculous things my parents have forwarded to my sister and me over the years, the Canadian email had been copied and pasted so many times it was difficult to follow the thread to its original source. But I did. It came from a right-wing outlet called the Conservative's Forum. A quick Google search shows its Twitter feed, but the site is either now defunct or most likely moved deeper into the dark recesses of the internet. In classic propaganda fashion, the email baits the

73

reader with one-sided takes on hot-button issues, but provides no follow-up, explanation, or support to back them up.

The email read like a redneck ballad, a good-old-boys' pact of international conservative solidarity by a Canadian troll who wished Trump was his prime minister. In regard to COVID, the Canadian says Trump asks a really good question: "Why aren't we using drugs that might work on people who are dying; what the hell do we have to lose?" The author neglects to mention Trump's overall disregard for science and his disdain for his chief medical advisor, Dr. Anthony Fauci. Neither was there any mention of Trump's asinine suggestion on national television that we might kill the coronavirus by injecting bleach into our veins.

I was so unnerved by the thought that not only were my parents okay with the junk in this email, but they were also celebrating it by forwarding to friends and family. I asked my sister about it, but she chided me for ringing the alarm bells at full volume. Just ignore it, she said. Not a chance.

> Dear Mom and Dad,
>
> When you forwarded this to me, I was a bit confused, then angry, and then disappointed. Why would you send this to ME? Then followed by, why would you send this to ANYBODY?
>
> Disappointed because this piece provides opinions with no supporting facts, no clear author or source (which I quickly found at Conservative's Forum), and is only filled with vitriol to fire-up Trump's base.
>
> And disseminating this type of garbage (some might even say propaganda) to friends and family is beneath you; you are so much better than this.
>
> Yes, you are fully free and entitled to send whatever type of political stuff you want to whomever you want. I just ask that you not send it to me anymore, unless there is some meat on it with facts and support—then I'm happy to discuss.

I could not let it slide. I had to call out my parents' email for what it was, and out of complete frustration, I also took the liberty to throw some shade their way. In response to the all-American White pride video, I attached a video clip of a compilation of young vocalists representing all ethnicities, genders, and races singing "All Good People" with lyrics reminding us that "we can't hold our breath forever when our brothers cannot breathe."[1] I hit "reply all" with a message that read, "This one is powerful, too. And such young voices." Nobody responded.

The Canadian email was so fraught with misinformation, but instead of pulling out my hair, I decided to work out some of my frustrations with a little creative writing. I turned every one of the author's half-truths into a creative exercise by using the Canadian's writing style and voice to set the record straight. For example, with the Canadian's comments about using untested drugs on dying COVID patients, my response went like this: *Whose life is so valuable that a little unproven, untested hydroxychloroquine pill wouldn't hurt? Go figure.*

But my favorite was the following:

> *The Canadian:* Trump is and has accomplished more than any U.S. President in my lifetime. (I'm seventy-even years old). He puts in eighteen-to-twenty-hour days. He isn't hiding in his office; he's out front—Briefing—ALL Americans almost every day.

> *My response:* If he's not hiding in his bunker during protests and American unrest, he's out front, all right. He may not have time to read his briefing reports about the Russian bounty placed on the heads of American soldiers, but heck, those eighteen-to-twenty-hour days he spends in front of Fox News or governing via Twitter is astounding. And speaking of hard work, just take a look at his golf game! I bet he's improved in the more than one-hundred-seventy times he's played already! You must be proud your hard-earned tax dollars contribute to his swing.

With all jesting aside, what that forwarded Canadian email did was give me a window into the political world in which my parents live. It's one thing to identify with the Republican party, but when my parents flippantly forward unhinged and potentially dangerous rhetoric to their peers, it's no wonder we have a news information crisis on our hands. My parents' circle of friends consists of highly educated and successful people with PhDs, medical degrees, and other advanced degrees. Yet they are collectively part of the problem. According to a study following the 2016 election, my parents' generation of people aged sixty-five and older "share most of the intentionally false or misleading news we see on social media."[2] So, what happened to their critical lens, or their moral filter, for that matter?

1. Vocal Rush, "All Good People" (Delta Rae Cover / Shelter in Place Edition).
2. Gebel, "Baby Boomers Share," lines 40–41.

The point is, chain emails—a digital form of propaganda—aren't about facts. What compels my parents to read, digest, and forward these conspiracy emails is how they make them feel. For more than two decades now, the "Clinton Body Bags"—a false email chain claiming former president Bill Clinton quietly did away with dozens of key witnesses who had evidence against him—became one of the original examples of a digital misinformation network. What was once urban legend, passed along by word of mouth, gained greater traction, longevity, and consequently an increased readership through chain emails: "yesterday's newspaper articles are forgotten with the next day's delivery, but e-mail lives forever."[3] The point of these chain emails is to embolden the faithful through fear and panic. It is our basic human nature to react when we feel threatened—a cornered cat is going to hiss. It's not surprising my parents didn't stop to think about the validity of the email's content or the ramifications of forwarding it when fear had already compelled them to hit the send button.

Unfortunately, my chiding about the Canadian email chain did nothing to convince them, as evidenced in their short response: "Sorry to offend you. You will not [be] bothered with our blather. We love you. Mom & Dad."

If this were a one-and-done, then maybe I could just dismiss it as "blather." Mere child's play. But the stakes got a little higher when my mother forwarded a video clip with the subject heading "Powerful Message." I could see the email's cyber traveling history; in typical Boomer fashion, this particular email had been forwarded nineteen times before it got to my inbox. With past recipients collected like trophies to testify to the content's validity and ultimate approval, my mother continued the practice and forwarded it to eleven more people, including me. With the video attachment came my mother's approval: "A friend sent this speech. Worthy of our listening." Obviously, this video is instantly credible because my mother trusts her friends only to share items worthy of attention. I wonder if it has ever dawned on my mother that the stuff her friends forward, no matter how much she likes and trusts them as people, still has the potential to be pure garbage? If it did, would she ever call them out for it?

The grainy and slightly out of focus video lasted a little under five minutes. In it a well-groomed White male teenager wearing a blue polo shirt with an American flag pin speaks behind a podium to presumably a public-school board of administrators about why he plans to leave his school to

3. Mikkelson, "Clinton Body Bags," lines 77–78.

attend a Christian one. He rails against the principal's attempts at diversity, equality, and inclusivity because, the boy confesses, "never once did he mention a race or identity that reflects me."[4] While the boy never mentioned CRT, he felt threatened when the narrative and educational landscape had the potential to no longer revolve around his White universe. And that was not acceptable to him. Nor, apparently, to my mother.

Absolutely flummoxed by this video and the fact that my own mother felt it worthy of our attention, I scrambled to find some answers. The problem is, my mother never mentions what precisely about this video is worthy. What are the boy's pearls of wisdom that I should garner? Is it that the gold standard of our American educational system—structured around the predominance and often exclusivity of the White people's narrative—for the first time in history, is being challenged in our public schools across the nation? Or is it that Black history *is American history* and needs to be taught honestly, completely, and more importantly *equally* in our classrooms? Or maybe the real rub for her is that some "woke" educators want to change the system entirely since "slavery is taught as the history of Black people and not the history of white people" (@TweetsByBilal)? Has my mother given serious thought about why specifically Black history and literature courses are considered "electives" and not essential "core" classes? What would happen if we make *Survey of Afro-American Literature* or *African American History: From Emancipation to the Present* graduation requirements for every high school student? Finally, what does Black History Month really say about our educational priorities?

All we're given in the video is a one-sided argument since we only hear the boy's perspective without any link to the principal's prior comments or school district policies. What I found most disturbing, however, is that the company that disseminated the video in question is far-right-wing media. A logo in the top right corner of the video identified the Daily Caller, a media outlet founded by Fox News host Tucker Carlson, one of CRT's most vocal opponents, who also happens to be one of my mother's former parishioners. Even power-house Episcopal churches harbor racists.

In high school back in the 1980s, well before the internet and digitized news sources, we used the old-fashioned library card catalogue for research. Once we scribbled the book's Dewey decimal number on paper, we then weaved through the stacks to find the matching number on the book's spine. We were taught to scrutinize our sources before working

4. Daily Caller, "Leftist Agenda in Class," Facebook video, July 31, 2021.

them into papers to support our thesis. If there's no named author, don't use it. If there's no publication information, don't trust it. Every quotation or paraphrase must be cited and connected to a reputable source—the very same system my dad used when writing his dissertation on the transmission of malaria by the female Anopheles mosquito. He knows the value of good, hard facts supported by solid data. His reputation as a scientist depended on it.

But as I connect the dots of emails and conversation snippets, it dawned on me pretty early in my awakening that the root of my family's disconnect over politics wasn't necessarily over ideologies or theologies, but rather plain old news and information. In October of 2020, still early in the pandemic, my parents joined us for a beach weekend to escape the monotony of the COVID lockdown. With both kids learning remotely, and after self-isolating for weeks, we felt renting a sanitized rental away from the fray was a safe way to be together.

Not knowing which way my parents were leaning in the upcoming election, I felt like an empty shell tossed among the waves. It was clear that my family had voted for Trump in 2016, but the stakes felt strangely higher for me with this next election. In 2016, the world didn't know much about Trump as a politician. Four years of chaos later, there should have been enough evidence to doubt his fitness for office. Did any of my impassioned pleas, carefully sourced articles, or corroborated statistics sway them? Had my letter resonated with them at all?

One month earlier, I sent my family a letter, my *magnum opus* of sorts. In it I laid out a series of my most compelling arguments against voting for Trump sprinkled with a few tough questions. I presented various reasons why Trump is unfit for the Oval Office, such as the documented rise in the number of hate crimes and White supremacists nationwide, his affinity to side with foreign dictators over our national security experts, and his alarming interest in White nationalism supposedly in the name of Christianity—just a summary of all the things I had been bringing to their attention over the previous four years. More importantly, I needed them to understand what was at stake with their votes, not just for the future of our country, but also for our family:

> I feel that the basic social mores and universal truths (i.e. dignity, decency, kindness, integrity, etc.) of how we judge a man (in this case the president) based on our Christian upbringing (loving our neighbor) have been ignored by my immediate family to

accommodate a political agenda. And that to me reeks of hypocrisy and has caused me to question what I thought to be a true,
moral, and a unifying foundation of our family.

My utter devastation now is that my family, whom I love
deeply, is considering aligning their beautiful Christian souls and
living testimony to a president who has an insatiable hunger for
White conservative "Christian" privilege at the expense of the
freedom and equality of others. I am broken when my family de-
fends this White president who beats the drums of nationalizing
our faith, who lusts for lying and bullying, who boasts about his
lack of responsibility, who testifies the rule of law and societal
mores don't apply to him, and finally, who takes pride in an unre-
pentant heart. Trump is no King David.

I am asking you to consider whether Trump, knowing what
we know now, is still the man for the job, for this America, for this
moment. There is a difference.

Therefore, I ask you, could Trump, even if he aligns with your
political views, be wrong for this country, so wrong that you would
put aside your party to heal our country?

My sister struggled and suggested that I was willing to "let our relationship go" over an election. I assured her I was not abandoning our
sisterhood. But what I could not bear, or even comprehend, was having
my Christian family support Trump for another term in office, and have
our family dynamic stay the same. It was not a threat, just a natural consequence of choices we make. Everything we valued, lived, and preached
was on the line with this vote. An unrealistic assertion? Perhaps. But
when I think back through history, I'm sure there were good, decent people much like ourselves in occupied Germany who agonized over family
members supporting Hitler. No, I'm not comparing Trump to Hitler. But
I am making the correlation that family systems have been and continue
to be divided by political choices.

Fifty-eight days before the 2020 election, my sister confessed she still
wasn't sure which way she would vote. I told her to take off her blinders and
she got defensive. If she had been paying attention, what more did she need
to know to make an informed decision? I mean, my God! I texted her with
a link to the PBS short film *Trump's American Carnage.*[5] The short film, now

5. Original funding for this program was provided by public television stations,
Corporation for Public Broadcasting, John D. and Catherine T. MacArthur Foundation,
Ford Foundation, Abrams Foundation, Park Foundation, Heising-Simons Foundation,
FRONTLINE Journalism Fund with major support from Jon and Jo Ann Hagler and

part of the larger Frontline documentary, traced the 45th president's abhorrent practice of name calling, shaming (especially the mockery of a disabled journalist), and dehumanizing rhetoric on his campaign trail.[6]

My sister actually watched it, and after inquiring several times for her response, she finally confessed what I had feared. She admitted she did watch the video, and in watching it, she was seeing footage for the first time. She was aghast at Trump's rhetoric, and in thinking back to how she could justify voting for Trump in 2016, she admits she chose to ignore the stuff she was hearing about him because it "made her feel uncomfortable." If she had seen the full picture of "the damage he was doing to people," she would not have voted for him. But because she didn't want "to get weighted [down]," she took her news from the margins and voted for him anyway.

In the end, my sister admitted she did not vote for Trump in 2020. She wouldn't say whether she voted for Biden, but frankly, I didn't care. I was just thankful she took her blinders off before the next election.

Although my dad had plenty of opportunity to talk during our walks on the beach, he finally opened up only after we all returned from the family getaway to our home. With bourbon in hand and under our patio umbrella with the evening sun beginning to set, he opened the discussion. Choosing his words slowly and carefully and diverting his eyes to the twirling ice in his glass, he admitted trying to write down his response to my *magnum opus* but, in the end, couldn't seem to get what he wanted to say down on paper.

I knew my dad had the capacity to vote with his conscience and not simply down the Republican party line because he told me as much. In 2016, he almost voted for Hillary Clinton, that is, until James B. Comey, then director of the Federal Bureau of Investigation, decided to reopen the investigation into her use of a private email server while she was U.S. Secretary of State. Comey's results *again* found no wrongdoing, but the mere suggestion that Hillary might have threatened our national security was just enough to tip my dad off the diving board back into the Republican pool.

If my dad feels convicted, he will act, even when it's hard or against the grain. When I was in high school, we attended Harriet Chapel, a small historic Episcopal church built in 1829.[7] I'm still not sure why my parents

---

additional support from Koo and Patricia Yuen.

6. Kirk, "Trump's American Carnage," January 26 and February 1, 2022.

7. Harriet Chapel, built for the workers of the Iron Furnace at Catoctin Mountain near Thurmont, Maryland, is registered as a historic site by the Daughters of the

felt a rural church well outside our community was better than a church we could walk to in town. It was quaint and intimate, that's for sure, and the twenty-minute drive on Route 15 through rolling hills and farm land was breathtaking. The rector, known to the parish affectionately as Father Schaefer, was a short, plump man with an unkept beard who wore Birkenstocks and looked more like a ZZ Top band member than a priest. He was earnest and kind, and during the Prayers of the People he prayed for each one of the hostages from the Lebanon Hostage crisis by name. Thanks to him, I know the name Terry Waite. The problem, however, was his preaching. I loved that he rarely used the lectern high above the congregation, preaching instead down among the people, which made the service intimate. The problem was his sermons lacked any substance as a result of little to no preparation. Most Sundays he'd fly by the cuff with a thought or two, and if we were lucky, he came prepared with a yellow sticky note adhered to the cover of his leather-bound prayer book.

This dereliction of duty incensed my dad. Because he was a preacher's kid, my dad could smell a rat. As a member of the vestry, an elected board that works as the liaison between the congregation and the clergy staff, my dad insisted he attend the College of Preachers in Washington, DC, for a refresh on writing sermons and hopefully to find some inspiration. Although the plan worked for a time, it wasn't long before Father Schaefer reverted back to his old ways. With Father Schaefer's lackluster sermons on the rise, my father, along with the majority of the vestry, had him ousted.

Giving his bourbon another swirl, Dad said he actually toyed with the idea of not voting in the 2016 election at all, but because our right to vote should never be taken for granted, felt he had to cast a ballot, even if it was for Trump. In 2020, I was hoping my father would be disgusted enough by Trump's performance as commander in chief once again to consider voting for a Democrat, if not with his conscience, at least with his gut.

As we sat, just the two of us, I listened intently, hopeful. To my great disappointment, my dad's defense of Trump ended up a jumbled mess of Fox News talking points—Biden has dementia, Biden's universal healthcare is the making of socialism, Biden is too old to serve—with no mention of Trump's own age, missteps, gross behavior, threat to our national security, or irresponsible handling of the pandemic. Not a word about any of that. My father's strongest personal conviction, delivered with a stiff back, disgust in his voice, and an incredulous brow, came courtesy of

---

American Revolution.

his University of Delaware fraternity brothers—many of them who had known Biden as a student more than a half-century earlier—who collectively agreed that his behavior as an undergraduate should bar him from ever being president. "Herd mentality's" finest hour.[8]

I'm not sure what was more disappointing, his shaky-at-best argument or the shakier sources upon which he based his justification for voting for Trump a second time. If his frat brothers were correct in asserting that Biden could not have improved as a human being and evolved into maturity and responsibility between his twenties and his seventies, then where does that place my dad and his antics as a student? For their argument to hold water, my dad's PhD should hit the shredder because he nearly flunked out of college his freshman year. Like two magnets, our conversation could not find a point of connection, no matter how hard we tried. My dad, still with drink in hand, walked a few feet to the highest point of our property and stared blankly into the woods. That was the end of our conversation.

Several months before our beach trip, I had sent my parents an email about sourcing our news consumption with intentionality. Since we're bombarded with news sound bites and headlines hundreds of times a day on our smart phones, I recommended AllSides.com, a news aggregator that uses scientific data to assess the political and ideological bias of various media outlets with the goal of exposing readers to news sources outside their "filter bubble." While not a perfect system, it does provide a benchmark about biases in the media:

> We have the tendency to look for news that supports our beliefs—
> that's human nature. And I admit I fall into that often. But how
> are we going to grow and learn and think if we are constantly fed
> by news that supports our current beliefs? All of us need to hear
> opposing views, see the facts/science/data, and use our brains to
> make informed decisions.

Based on my dad's justifications for supporting Trump again in 2020, it was clear to me my father hadn't considered AllSides. When he sent me an article headlined "Message from God" from the *Epoch Times*, I sent another email about our choice of news, but this time more impassioned and direct:

> Discussions around politics for the two of us has not been easy
> because we are not dealing with the same deck of cards (hence

8. Lee, "Trump Says," lines 5–6.

my attempt at a book discussion). And I think that is in large part because we get our information from different sources.

Would you be willing, alongside me, to modify your news absorption with intentionality? Unsubscribe from far-right media and strive to read, watch, and listen to middle of the road?

Again, my father never responded. I grew up in a home where Fox *was* the news. Unfortunately, I've noticed my dad's Republican stridence increase over time and with age, much like Jen Senko's father in her 2015 American documentary *The Brainwashing of My Dad*. Long before Kellyanne Conway introduced the notion of "alternate facts" into our lexicon and popular consciousness, Roger Alies' Fox News media machine was churning out propaganda and luring folks such as my father hook, line, and sinker. While I had removed Facebook from my phone—on a dare from my kids, a feat they were sure I could never pull off successfully— and switched from CNN/MSNBC nightly news to the PBS Newshour and BBC News, my father continues apace his news consumption at Fox and with stacks of the *Epoch Times* piled next to his favorite chair. I hope he reads from other sources. But I see the Fox News app on his phone, the saved bookmarks on his laptop, and most disappointingly, I hear their twisted talking points come from his own lips.

Old habits die hard. The hope of moving the needle of his right-leaning news consumption to the middle is really quite ridiculous on my part. There is great satisfaction in placing our trust in broadcasters whose voices, like that of a familiar friend, sound comforting and believable. In the end, I'm not surprised that Trump was still the lesser of two evils for my dad. Trump's dismantling of our national security, his abysmal handling of the COVID pandemic, and his various abuses—supposedly in the name of Christianity but blatantly for political gain—did not sway my father. Neither did Trump's caustic behavior and lack of plain human decency. That was the hardest pill to swallow.

10

The Holy Grail

We need to stop just pulling people out of the river. We need to go upstream and find out why they're falling in.

—Archbishop Desmond Tutu

The path to Auschwitz was paved with indifference.

—Ian Kershaw

Completely dejected by my failure to reach my family before the 2020 election, I was determined to find something—with even more authority—to shake my family out of their complacent stupor, or whatever it was that enabled their continued support for Trump. I came out swinging from 2020 even more zealous, determined to prove to myself, if no one else, that I wasn't crazy. Years ago, my sister mentioned the world of Brené Brown, an American research professor who studies shame, vulnerability, and leadership. I've never read her books, but I stumbled upon her *Unlocking Us* podcasts during my self-induced therapeutic walking sessions.

In scrolling the library of her podcasts on Spotify, the segments about dehumanization and leadership caught my attention. With earbuds in place, I hit play and began my journey down the road. It wasn't long before something clicked. What Brown was saying was exactly what I had been trying to articulate. And she had research, data, credentials, expertise, and humor to back it all up—this was it, the Holy Grail. I couldn't walk home fast enough. I started to jot down notes, but every word seemed too important to exclude. I hit rewind for a third listen, and ended up transcribing both segments word for word.

There's something about typing out each word that connects it to meaning for me. The repetitive stop–type–rewind–play of sentence fragments every few seconds meant Brown's words burrowed deep into my mind and heart. Once I finished the transcriptions—no surprise here!—I sent them to my family members and asked the following questions because my struggle wasn't over:

Prior to the 2020 election, I asked two tough questions:

1. Could Trump, even if he aligns with your political views, be wrong for the country, so wrong that you would put aside your party line to heal our nation?

2. Where is your line in the sand? Do you have a line in the sand?

You may think this is water under the bridge since Biden is now in office. I think we all know these weighty issues go deeper than an election cycle. My need for this understanding is for when Trump runs again in 2024, and my family potentially jumps back on the bandwagon, or for when another Trump-like (Democrat or Republican) candidate tries to run for office in the future. As Republicans, you must answer these questions since your party is fighting between two clear and opposing factions: The old Grand Old Party and QAnon/conspiracy-toting Trump loyalists.

In the first podcast about power and leadership, Brown talks about four kinds of power, but zeroes in on what she calls "Power Over" and "Power With."[1] The goal of leaders using Power Over is "to leverage fear, divide, destabilize, and to devalue decency as a sign of weakness," and she places Trump and his administration in this camp.[2] The other end of the spectrum is Power With, where the goal is "to leverage connection and empathy, to unite and stabilize."[3] One of the main tools of Power Over is creating fear, and the way "to maintain Power Over is by demonstrating an ever-increasing capacity for cruelty, including shaming, bullying, belittling—especially toward vulnerable populations," Brown said.[4] The exact technique the head of school used in his morning staff devotionals to maintain power and order over me and the other teachers.

1. Brown, "Brené on Words," January 13, 2021.
2. Brown, "Brené on Words," January 13, 2021.
3. Brown, "Brené on Words," January 13, 2021.
4. Brown, "Brené on Words," January 13, 2021.

Brown later defines this technique, in her discussion about shaming, as "dehumanization"—"demonizing the enemy, making them less than human, and thus not worthy of humane treatment."[5] Trump employed this very tactic when describing the mothers, fathers, and children crossing our southern border as "infestations," "animals," "aliens," "rapists," and "thugs."

In one of the few face-to-face political conversations I've had with my mother, I pressed the issue of separating families at our southern border. She said the problem of immigration is complicated, implying there is no easy solution, and that no president has been able to solve it. I agreed. I then asked her how separating children from their parents is a viable solution, my voice rising to reflect the absurdity of it all. My mother shifted the conversation away from Trump's despicable border policies to "those mothers." I listened. My mother went on to rebuke "those mothers" who "give their children away" to the *coyotes* who illegally smuggle them into the United States.

"Who gives her child away to strangers?" she said, followed by, "What kind of mother does that?"

"A very desperate one," I answered.

I didn't understand it then, but after absorbing Brown's podcasts, I began to see the markings of dehumanization in my mother's response. Instead of showing a shred of empathy and understanding about what type of deplorable circumstances would bring mothers to hand their children over to strangers—to truly step inside her shoes and walk around in them a bit—my mother turned those very mothers into villains. "Those women" suggests a different type of mother, one who is more abusive than loving, more ignorant than desperate, more criminal than merciful. I told my mother that I couldn't image the level of desperation it would take for a mother to reach the point where the best option for a better future for her children was to hand them—and her life's saving—over to a human trafficker.

"We've never experienced that type of fear and hopelessness," I told my mother. "They have very little protection from abuse, drug lords, and abject poverty. I can't image how bad it must be before you decide to travel hundreds of miles, often on foot, for just the chance of a better life." Rather than seeing such action as the ultimate sacrifice, to give up one's life for another, my mother saw it as criminal behavior.

5. Brown, "Brené on Words," January 13, 2021.

I don't know how to solve our immigration problem since there are so many variables that contribute to its existence. But I do know this: I will not stand idly by and allow any politician to convince us that separating families is a solution acceptable to a healthy democracy. Nor will I accept my family's indifference to the heinous practice because it was Obama who built the cages. If we deem "those mothers" as "other" and separate from the rest of humanity, then it makes Trump's border policy that much more palatable. Even for Christians. And I'm pretty sure this is why my family remained silent on this issue. Finally, there was a president willing to take the hard stand on immigration and give those animals, those infestations, those rapists, and those mothers their just desserts.

At the end of that immigration conversation with my mother, no doubt exasperated by my relentless pushing, she wagged her finger at me and asked, "And what are *you* doing?" The question was maddeningly compelling. On one level, it's a fair question—I interpreted it to mean what am I doing to make this world a better place? But with her gesticulation and her emphasis on "you," there was another level, seasoned with a healthy dose of skepticism, about whether I was actually doing anything worthwhile.

Since ministering to others, especially those in need, is the closest thing to godliness, my parents' resume of volunteerism—from clothing donations to food pantries to soup kitchens—shames the rest of us. They are always outwardly "doing" something. My mom's finger-wagging question was a deflection of sorts. It moved the conversation away from the immigration issue and squarely onto me.

I had seen this technique before with my brother-in-law, Tim, on the same topic of immigration. Instead of continuing the difficult conversation, he changed the subject by implying that what I have in passion, I lack in bandwidth—an incredibly patronizing comment that hurt me deeply. He buttered me up as his favorite sister-in-law, then maintained our relationship was "way more important" so as to ensure receiving a future Christmas present from me than it was for him to enlighten me with his counterarguments. He was content to dismiss me and chose the easy way out by agreeing to disagree. To his credit, he later apologized to me in person, but we have not talked politics since then.

What this told me is that Tim was perfectly fine with Trump "doing his job" by applying "the law" (i.e., jailing parents) since to do anything less would, in essence, be breaking the law. He saw this action as a symbol of American strength meted out by a strong-arm president who was actually doing something radical about our immigration issues, especially when no other president before him was willing to do likewise. The separation of children was a byproduct of the parents breaking the law in the first place. If they didn't come, there would be no separation. Blame falls squarely on those parents. For avoiding corruption and possible death. For wanting basic necessities, such as food and clean water. For seeking an honest livelihood to support their families. For desiring to live in peace and not fear. Permanently taking children from their parents, and often intentionally transporting them to disparate parts of the United States, far from the southern border, was a better solution for Trump than deporting the whole family unit back to their country of origin. So much for family values.

This notion of elevating the strong man had been gaining popularity in fundamentalist and evangelical circles for decades. This pseudo-sexy brand of theology, according to "The Rise and Fall of Mars Hill" podcast, looked like pastors with iPads wearing skinny jeans and lacing their sermons with occasional f-bombs. True men answer to no one but God and hold their families in the balance. Women submit. Macho Jesus knocks out the humble one. Because this wave of toxic Christian masculinity had already taken root across the evangelical world, Trump strategically stepped into that persona and the embrace of the majority of evangelicals. Trump calls the shots and doesn't care who ends up as collateral damage. The dye had already been cast. And Trump doesn't care. End of story.

I did not know anything about this movement in evangelicalism, sometimes referred to as "toxic masculinity," because it was not my world. For evangelicals such as Mark Driscoll, Christian author and former founder of Mars Hill Church in Seattle (not the Mars Hill in Michigan founded by Wheaton College alumnus Rob Bell), the Scottish knight and fourteenth-century freedom fighter William Wallace—and specifically, Mel Gibson's portrayal of Wallace in his 1995 film *Braveheart*—became a popular archetype for Christian masculinity. My brother-in-law will tell you that's one of his favorite movies. Gibson's Wallace became the embodiment of an unapologetic warrior in the conservative movement's battles in America's culture wars, complete with a rallying cry: "I know you can fight, but it's our wits that make us men!" Driscoll even chose the pseudonym "William Wallace II" as his private chat handle in his church's discussion boards so he could express his misogynistic, unorthodox, and toxic views anonymously (and freely).[6] If husbands were abusive or un-

6. Evans, "Inside Mark Driscoll's Disturbed Mind," July 29, 2014.

faithful to their partners, the wife was to blame. He didn't care if women were abused and relationships broken, because overlooking a moral framework is acceptable if it accomplished a greater good—like increasing church membership with newly converted souls.

Anticipating the end of yet another heated and unproductive conversation with my mother, I paused before I answered her question. I understood completely the implied guilt attached to her inquiry. My sister had adopted three biracial children and worked in full-time church ministry, while all I had to show for my commitment to racial justice was a few months of working with a refugee nonprofit. I told my mother that I was attempting to figure out how we got to this fractured place culturally in the United States, and that I was trying to make up for lost time because I hadn't been paying attention to politics much before the 2015 general election. But I was paying attention now. I'd spent countless hours reading, researching, talking, and asking questions. It was eye-opening and tough work for me. I was exhausted from absorbing and processing as much as I could as quickly as I could. But because I had nothing to "show" for the effort, it suddenly felt hollow and inconsequential. I wrote about it anyway.

Growing up, I wish my parents had emphasized civics with my sister and me, including intentional conversations about who they voted for and why. Perhaps if it had been one of those uncomfortable but necessary "talks," similar to the birds and the bees, I might have grasped its importance years earlier than I finally did. In my family of origin, voting was treated as a deeply private matter that you didn't ask or talk about in polite conversation, much like taboos about asking about someone's weight or sex life.

I wish I had learned the correlation between Christian duty and our voting practices—how they must work in tandem. Is it America's goal to keep filling our food pantries with day-old bread or to make these types of social services obsolete because, as the richest country in the world, we actually made it a priority to end hunger? Getting to that place has everything to do with whom we vote into office. In other words, if we are content to spend hours in a soup kitchen and vote for politicians who aren't actively working to eradicate poverty (and everything that falls under that umbrella, like healthcare, education, and voting rights) then we're nothing more than do-gooders with White savior complexes, happier to keep folks in their place of need than actually to effect real change.

Before the political conversations closed entirely with my brother-in-law, he did graciously answer my question about his line in the sand. Tim told me very early in my awakening that he does not pay attention to what Trump says or tweets because "all politicians lie." What he cares about, he says, is Trump's record; that how he reaches the goal doesn't matter, as long as he gets there. While Trump made him uncomfortable, Tim says he could live with him as long as he champions his conservative political causes.

While this conversation predated the January 6 Capitol riot, my response foreshadowed what might become of our country if we continued to ignore what Trump says:

> What your method lacks is integrity and balance, one that should hold the stature of his character as equally important as his policy—a tenant of conservatism, I believe. Would you buy a house after selectively looking at only one or two rooms?
>
> How nice it must be to flip the switch and dismiss what Trump says—his fear mongering, conspiracy toting, racist, and hate–filled jabs in his tweets and interviews—the likes of which we've never seen from someone holding the highest office. How convenient that you can brush his uncouth and bristly parts aside and accept that's just who he is. How refreshing it must be to wear political blinders that allow you to stay laser-focused on your issues while dismissing his chatter that is bruising our wonderful nation.
>
> Because when you ignore his unbecoming behavior and what he says, you are in essence condoning it. You may see your support for Trump as claiming the higher moral ground because you are standing firm on the political topics that ring true to your convictions. You might argue that your morality and charity are tightly wrapped in your list of political topics, and Trump is merely the vehicle to get you there. In the end it will all be justified it if we can get one more conservative judge, ban abortion, and lower taxes.
>
> But at what cost?
>
> Maybe the real moral high ground is setting aside your political identity and choosing compassion for our nation that is unraveling.
>
> I think you would agree that this president is like no other, and because of this, we can't dismiss his divisive behavior as an irrelevant side show. We need a leader more than ever for all of our citizens. The level of hatred, divide, and pain is off the chart, and I don't see Trump doing one damn thing in his words or deeds to relieve the suffering of the American people.

I don't know how Tim feels about Trump since January 6, or if he views the 2020 election as fair or "stolen." Nor do I know if he puts any credence in the importance of what Trump says. But if he stands by his voting formula, then voting for Trump in 2024 will be a sure thing since, for him, the "ability of a candidate to implement the solutions needed to fix the issues in our country is the most important reason for my vote." Morality plays no role in Tim's vote because morals are subjective: "How do we truly know the character of a person," he asks, adding, "How can we say one person is right and another is wrong?" No need for moral absolutes, just keep moving the goal posts.

As for Tim's line in the sand, he has two priorities when he votes at the polls. He will *not* vote for a candidate who (1) supports abortion or (2) "promises to implement policies that disadvantage minority citizens." I'm not surprised abortion is Number One on his list since, for most Republicans, abortion is the *only* issue. I was three years old when Roe v. Wade became law. Because Trump finally tipped the balance of the Supreme Court back to conservatives, which consequently opened the door to up-end abortion, Trump, according to the religious right, is without-a-doubt concrete evidence of God's plan working out in our lifetime. According to evangelical Republicans, he is helping us get one step closer to a true Christian nation. No wonder Trump's base unabashedly refers to him as the Messiah. But what people like my brother-in-law fail to acknowledge (or at least say out loud) is that, on the other hand, Trump also eroded our culture by replacing Truth with "fake news," and by making a mockery of our society's standards and the mores that we had deemed necessary to hold our democracy together.

Now the abortion topic requires its own volume, but whatever we think of the complex issues surrounding that subject, the urgent question that Trump forces us all to ask is this: Is having a president who wears the "pro-life" mantle (albeit only in order to win conservative votes rather than from personal conviction) enough to justify his presidency if he doesn't abide by the Constitution, our checks and balances, and/or the rule of law? An authoritarian president who abandons these civic mores is far more dangerous to our republic than abortion. Playing by the rules matters for future generations:

> We must defend our Constitution because *precedent matters.*
> What we do today shapes what the other side will do to us tomor-
> row. We have to play by the rules if we want them to respect the

rules when they are in power. There is no way our side will stay in power forever. Someday, our political opponents will control the White House and both chambers of Congress. When they do, we will rue the day we traded away the Constitution's guardrails.[7]

But with the help of Trump's three fast-tracked conservative U.S. Supreme Court justices, and the overturning of Roe v. Wade in the summer of 2022, my guess is Tim feels vindicated in voting for Trump. One hundred percent. But does Tim not feel a twinge of regret for the constitutional crisis resulting from voting for Trump in 2016 and 2020? Is there no buyer's remorse since Trump's attempted coup on January 6, 2021? Is there no outrage when Trump's divisiveness fuels the fire burning the GOP to the ground? If Trump is the Republican nominee in 2024, as seems likely, will Tim finally see that Trump is *not* a political candidate but rather the authoritarian leader of a dangerous political movement?

Tim's second line in the sand about "minority citizens" is what perplexes me most. Let's just take voting laws. I've tried to talk with him about voter suppression, but the only thing he is willing to discuss is the argument for voter ID, an argument he claims has bipartisan support. I mentioned some of the new voter suppression bills and tactics employed by the Republicans, but he won't acknowledge or discuss any of them. Just voter ID. In my state of North Carolina, I am not required to provide ID to vote[8] *and* we have no voter fraud or impropriety—the voter ID argument is smoke and mirrors, as I tried to explain to my sister:

> The bottom line is this: Republicans can't win an election in a state like Georgia (or my own state of North Carolina) unless they cheat. And how do they cheat? They look at the data from the last election in which they lost and pinpoint ways to suppress the vote in that district for the next election. How? Limit voting. Reduce the days of early voting, remove/reduce weekend voting since that's really the only time that the working class can afford to vote, reduce the number of polling stations in rural areas, remove drop boxes, even make it illegal to hand out free food and water to those waiting in hours-long lines . . . the list goes on.
>
> If Republicans were really interested in fair and free elections, they would first acknowledge that 2020 was a legitimate election, and second, that all votes count and should therefore make it

7. Miller, "Convict Trump," lines 64–68.

8. North Carolina conservative justices reinstated voter ID laws; therefore, registered voters are now required to show a valid ID at the polls in 2023.

easier for their constituents to vote. The voter ID argument is only cover for a deeply rooted practice that serves to systematically disenfranchise the least among us.

In 2020 we had the highest voter turnout in history, thanks largely to BIPOC folks showing up at the polls. Unfortunately, instead of celebrating because of a well-oiled and functioning democracy, Republicans introduced more than 440 bills with provisions that restrict voting access in forty-nine states in the 2021 legislative sessions.[9] When we look at what's happening in key swing states, it looks like voter suppression bills are moving us back to the Jim Crow era.

There is no proof of rampant voter fraud anywhere in the United States. The Cyber Ninjas hired by Republicans haven't found any. Trump-appointed local and federal judges have found nothing. Even the conservative stalwart Heritage Foundation thinktank says as of 2022, there have only been 1,353 individual incidents of proven voter fraud in the entire country[10]—and some of that fraud was carried out by Republicans themselves. Republicans have masterfully created voter fraud hysteria, encouraged and perpetuated by Trump's megaphone, which claims that out of the more than 168 million registered voters, we need to protect the integrity of the vote by tightening laws specifically targeting minority and rural populations. The punishment does not fit the (statistically negligible) crime.

The final and most unwavering variable in my brother-in-law's voting formula is party allegiance. Our duty as American citizens, according to Tim, is to vote—a belief we both share. He argues his vote must reflect the party that shares his vision for what's best for America, and historically that has been the Republican party. So far, his logic makes perfect sense. Therefore, Tim argues his "only option" is to vote for the candidate put forward by that party, since "supporting Trump and voting Republican are two totally different things." And here's where I begin to scratch my head. With all of Trump's baggage of impeachments and indictments, is this Republican frontrunner really Tim's *only* option? If his answer is yes, then political party definitely plays a higher role than what's best for this country, and that's just plain dangerous.

I heard the same party allegiance argument from Mitch McConnell when a reporter asked then Senate minority leader about his moral red line. The reporter asked McConnell to explain how months earlier, he had

9. Brennan Center for Justice, "Voting Laws Roundup," December 21, 2021.
10. Heritage Foundation, "Sampling of Recent Election Fraud Cases."

condemned Trump for his actions and involvement in the deadly January 6 attacks as a "dereliction of duty" and held him "practically and morally responsible," but now says he'd support him enthusiastically if he is the Republican presidential nominee in 2024.[11] There is no moral dilemma for McConnell because, as my brother-in-law implied, partisan priorities take precedence over what's best for the United States. Tim's voting formula, which provides all the guardrails to stay inside that framework, looks something like this:

> Rule No. 1: Abortion + party loyalty + amorality = his Republican vote

> Rule No. 2: Any number multiplied by zero is always zero.

While my initial anxiety about my family was based on a moral disconnect, I see now I have crossed the political Rubicon by questioning their party of choice. Please help me understand how you can vote Republican, with its systemic voter suppression tactics, if your second line in the sand is about protecting and safeguarding people of color? How do you justify limiting anyone's vote? I mean, it's comical. Except it's not. Because the only way to make this argument work is if you truly believe Trump's Big Lie, that voter fraud is rampant, and therefore it is your duty to save America and tighten the laws to "protect" the voting process by limiting the other party's vote.

It's also very possible I missed the point of Tim's second line in the sand entirely. Maybe he defines "minority" to mean something very different. Many Christians believe they are a persecuted minority. For Christians around the globe in countries such as India, China, and North Korea, this is often the case. But in America, White Christians complain that their victimization comes from "a broad secularist and leftist persecution" because "the world is a place inhospitable to their gospel."[12] Dr. Steven Woodburn, a college friend and history professor, said in a text to me that "it's not surprising White people confuse being a declining majority with being a persecuted minority, especially when these same folks feel threatened by affirmative action."

It never dawned on me to ask Tim for clarification about how he defines "minority citizen." I instinctively understood "minority citizen" to mean people of color and other marginalized groups. Could it be that when Tim speaks of "minority citizens," he has mostly himself or the

11. Benen, "Why McConnell Struggled," lines 31–33.

12. Corrigan, "Why Do White Christians," line 11.

future of his group in mind? Pluralism, multiculturalism, and women's rights, among other things, have the potential to not only threaten what "Make[s] America Great," but most importantly, to weaken the very core of White American male power.

My guess is many of my family members will vote for Trump in 2024 because the formula allows for it. And Tim's argument that "supporting Trump and voting Republican are two totally different things" is a total cop-out. It's splitting hairs, because if you tick the box for Trump, you are effectively supporting him because he is not horrendous enough to lose your vote.

11

I Choose Her

Now, every time I witness a strong person; I want to know: What dark did you conquer in your story? Mountains do not rise without earthquakes.

—@Katherine MacKenett

I n June 2020, a few weeks before my daughter's sixteenth birthday, another shoe dropped.

I was standing at the kitchen sink, looking out the window at our pool where my daughter and a friend were swimming. I could hear the girls splashing and their laughter outside, but when it grew quiet, I stopped washing dishes and glanced outside. I saw Claire and her friend floating in the water, embracing, tenderly and affectionately, and speaking in hushed voices. And I knew. As I stood motionless, all the pieces began to fit together.

When Claire was four or five years old, she came bounding into the kitchen like she had something important on her mind. She told me she tried to tell her friends that she was a boy, but they wouldn't believe her. Her frustration at their disbelief almost unglued her. I stopped fixing sandwiches, looked at her with a puzzled expression, and told her matter-of-factly that she was not a boy. She was born with all the "girl parts." She stormed off in a dramatic huff, pig tails bouncing. And that was that. End of discussion.

How I wish I knew then what I know now. A lifetime of regrets in that single moment. I wish I had had the insight to scoop her up and ask her to tell me more. Did she really feel like a boy, or was it that she just didn't like dresses and other girly things? Either way, we would figure it out together. Promise.

Claire has never been one to fall into conventionalism. She showed more interest in LEGOs and Matchbox cars than Barbie dolls and unicorns, yet somehow girly things still made it under the Christmas tree, even if they were not by her request. She's worn hats of every color and brim since she figured out how to put them on her head. She wanted to play league football but settled for lacrosse when she saw the Bishop Ireton High School boys team playing on the field behind our house in Alexandria, Virginia. The disappointment was palpable when she learned that women's lacrosse does not come with the same gear. She plays the drums. And basketball. And she wants nothing to do with pink. She is as *bona fide* a tomboy as Scout Finch.

Claire loathes dresses, yet I forced her to wear one every day when she was a student at Trinity. The second year I taught there, we decided the kids would attend, too. Both of my kids still have visceral reactions when reflecting on that year. My son got in trouble multiple times for using the word "frick," as in "what the frick," a made-up word in a harmless expression, yet he was shamed publicly and punished for using it. Claire was miserable, too. I had no idea, and no one thought to tell me until the end of the school year. Apparently, Claire cried every day. Her kindergarten teacher tried everything under the sun to help her, and even went against protocol by allowing her to wear her favorite brown knitted bear hat for security. She'd worn it so much the eyes fell off. When that didn't work, my husband and I finally were summoned in late spring for a meeting with the principal, Mrs. Anger. (Not a pseudonym.)

The meeting was filled with pleasantries and niceties, and a few anecdotes to give us some insight into Claire's discontent. The kind of conversation where you don't see the bottom line until after the fact because it's so covered in fluff. It wasn't until after the meeting that my husband and I regurgitate back to each other what we just heard. Once we put it all together, according to Mrs. Anger, Claire was not a good fit, and there was nothing more they could do to help her. "Not all children are meant for this private school," she said. I couldn't have agreed more. And it was this incident—spoken to my face, that my daughter was not enough—that served as the impetus to seek a fresh start in not only a new school, but also a new state. Never again would I darken the door of another Christian school.

After watching Claire and her friend in the pool that afternoon, I told my husband. Before we could sit down for our family meeting later that evening, in her nervousness, Claire blurted out, "Is this meeting about me being gay?" Because the political circus already had taken up residence in my head for several years, I felt unmoored, my emotional energy nearly tapped. The word *anxious* comes to mind. Also, *vulnerable*. *Raw*, even. My husband also wondered how Claire's revelation might change his life, but quickly realized the selfishness in that response—it was not about us.

"Are you sure?" I asked Claire, then proceeded to suggest another possibility. "You are so young, maybe you'll change your mind when you get older?"

She shook her head, and I started to cry.

Claire said she knew her sexual orientation was different around eighth grade. But she didn't have the vocabulary, or the confidence, to talk about it, so, eventually, she decided to just show us. In her own way and in her own time. She wasn't afraid to tell us, because we've always been vocal supporters of the rights of all people, especially the marginalized. She felt safe, but she knew the conversation would be hard. And hard things give her anxiety. As a youngster, it once took Claire all afternoon to apologize when she hit me with a ball. I knew she didn't mean to do it, but it still stung. I waited for a good forty-five minutes before she could admit she did it and was sorry. And her little body, emotionally exhausted yet utterly relieved, just folded in my arms. Pride runs deep in this family tree.

Her brother, home from Dartmouth College because of the COVID pandemic, eventually joined our meeting. I turned to Claire and told her she needed to tell him.

"Tell me what?" Noah asked. "What's going on?"

Claire hesitated, but as he stood patiently waiting, she eventually gathered up courage. For the first time, tears filled her eyes and flowed when he bear-hugged her and told her he always knew. He assured her it was alright, and he was proud of her, and that he loved her. And siblings bonded when the vulnerable bravery of my daughter met the unadulterated acceptance of my son. It was beautiful.

I cried, too. But my tears came from a collection of deep places. First and foremost was a place of want. After having my son, the notion of infertility issues before baby number two was not on my radar. I didn't even know that was a thing. But there it was, and I was it. That lonely road toward pregnancy became my new obsession. After years, and a miscarriage, and rounds of vitamins and vaginal suppositories, my Trinidadian obstetrician, who spoke with a cadence and dialect that sounded like swaying palm trees, sent me to a specialist. With self-injections to promote ovulation and a petri dish later using my husband's sperm, half of Claire's DNA was artificially inseminated into my womb. And she's been a fighter ever since. During one of those early appointments, when you haven't told the world about the pregnancy for fear of jinxing it, my doctor couldn't find her heartbeat. An immediate appointment with another specialist caught me from free-falling into ugly despair. With my husband present, and a vaginal ultrasound, we found her, and her heartbeat was loud and clear. I finally exhaled. Strong willed, stubborn, opinionated; she beats her own drum. And I wouldn't have it any other way.

With her birth, our family was now complete. A son and a daughter. I needed nothing else. And like most mothers, I thought about the future for both of my kids and those milestone moments that fill a photo album: graduations, driver's licenses, first loves, weddings—how I will have to pick up the pieces of her dad when that day arrives. So, my tears also came from this place of dreams—*my dreams*. Dreams of what I thought my daughter's future would look like. There will be love, no doubt, but since Claire removed dresses from her wardrobe years ago, I won't ever see her in that white gown. Even my son acknowledged, with a twinge of sadness I believe, that if she marries, there will not be another man in the family. Same life stage, just different scenes. A reframing for me, but not an end.

The bulk of my tears, however, sprung from the saddest and most fragile place of my being. Still trying to maneuver contentious communications and unresolved conflict with my family, how on earth could those relationships bear this news? My family should have been a bedrock for me and a place of refuge, not the hot, shifting sands it was. Because I didn't know how to navigate a way forward for myself with them, let alone a way forward with them and my gay daughter, I begged her to let us know when she was ready to tell the extended family. The next day, I started Googling "how to support a gay child." One of the podcasts I found taught me that my initial response, about growing out of gayness like it was some temporary fad, was a microaggression. Strangely enough, there was an odd comfort in learning my response was not unique. I heaped apologies upon Claire as I held her, promising that I'll learn everything I can about this new world.

Another tidbit I learned came from Instagram. In it a gay woman gave the argument that she never "came out" with a formal declaration because her heterosexual siblings and cousins never had to "come out" as straight. Why should she? A "coming out" normalizes the stigmatization of an already marginalized group. Claire liked that idea. The problem is, however, when you're not fully out, in whatever form that takes, you and your family are still in hiding. It's probably even harder because you have to take inventory of who is an ally and who's not. Claire's friends on the traveling lacrosse team at her high school know. While other parents posted prom pictures, I was forbidden from doing so. When do I get to celebrate all of my daughter, and not just bits and pieces? When can she live in the full expression of herself? I resent that this hiding gives my family of origin the upper hand. This is not sustainable.

I'm pretty sure my family suspects Claire is gay. My dad gets nosey about boys and boyfriends and my mother wonders why she doesn't wear dresses anymore. They haven't come right and out asked it, I think, because they're afraid of the answer. Afraid because they'll eventually remember all the homophobic comments they said around the table not knowing that their gay granddaughter, whom they love, absorbed every hurtful word like burning coals heaped upon her head. And my God, if they suspected her sexual orientation but said those things anyway . . . Lord help them.

I'm sure I'll get blamed for part of this at some point. If I had only told them ahead of time, they would have been more selective with their words. As painful and as shocking as it was to hear them verbalize their opinions, I'm glad they did so out in the open. First, there are witnesses. And now we know exactly where they stand; the decision is on them about what to do with it all. Growing up, my parents made every attempt to show fairness to my sister and me. We each got the same number of gifts under the Christmas tree, and the same educational support. In addition, my mother would buy things in twos. For example, when living overseas, she selected two wool oriental rugs. I guess she figured that when they were dead and buried there would be enough to divide between us that she wanted to make some of that process easier. While life is far from fair, my parents really did strive for egalitarianism. Will that same theory apply to Claire? Will my mom revisit Scripture to figure out a way to love her granddaughter unconditionally and equally with the other grandchildren? Will she perform the wedding service like she's done for many of my cousins? Will my dad come to her wedding, just send a gift, or do nothing at all?

Claire told us she has no desire to tell the family. Who could blame her? She told us that if they ever asked, she wants us to speak on her behalf. She gave us her blessing, and we gave her our word. "What if they don't love me the same, and what if they change toward me?" she asked. What was so heart-wrenchingly sad is I have no assurances to give her. I don't know how the family will respond. I really don't know. Based on what they've already said about gay weddings and Scripture, which they feel supports their beliefs, I think this has the potential to break the branches. That is not my desire.

However, I've already told Claire, if I must choose—something I am fully prepared to do—I will always choose her.

12 _____

In Deep

> To show compassion for an individual without showing concern
> for the structures of society that make him an object of compas-
> sion is to be sentimental rather than loving.
>
> —William Sloane Coffin Jr.

When my anger and disillusionment reached its apex, Mom told me I
should consider divorcing the family.

As startled as I was to hear her suggest such a thing, I had used that
exact expression with my liberal, Seattle-based cousin just not long before
the 2020 election. In an out-of-the-blue instant message, my cousin had
asked me whether my father was voting for Trump. When I told her that my
father—and the rest of my family of origin as well—likely would vote for
Trump, she said if she were in my shoes, she "would have a much more difficult time being understanding." I told her most days it felt like an identity
crisis, but increasingly, it felt more "like a divorce."

Divorce is the last stop in a relationship. It's an acknowledgment that
the relationship is irreparably broken. Yet even if it's officially dissolved, the
parties remain partially yoked because of "the kids." In my case, grandkids
are involved. It requires a delicate balance of privacy and civility, boundaries and birthday parties. A regrouping. Even though I was the catalyst for
the divorce, were my family members truly honest, they would acknowledge how each one of them has contributed to our estrangement. No matter
the assignation of blame, all of us are left holding the pieces and wondering
how it might be put back together, if it ever can be.

My parents' refusal to talk about what's been going on the last several years means there's been no formal declaration of separation, and no guidelines for navigating our future interactions. Without boundaries, it's awkward and disconcertingly quiet. One thing is certain: our relationship has changed. We call less frequently, and when we do, it's usually just me and my mom talking about the kids. She feels connected if she knows what's on our calendar.

As I started grappling with our new rhythm of family dynamics, trying to find my place without emotional proximity, my mother once again sent a group email with a link included. The subject line said: "Biden sets sights on education," and like her other group emails, she indicated the value of the linked article, yet never explicitly articulated her intention in sending it. As a former educator, I am, of course, interested in what Biden is doing to improve our education systems. This article, however, was not that. Not one bit. Instead, it showed me exactly what I wasn't looking for—proof that my years of attempting to reach my parents had come to naught. The only thing I had to show for my efforts was an ever-widening divide.

My mother sent this email the day before my daughter and I left for a lacrosse tournament in Pennsylvania. Because I was preparing for our road trip, I didn't pay much attention to the email and figured I'd read it when I had more time. This was one of the few tournaments close enough to family that it gave us the rare opportunity to stay at my sister's home instead of in a hotel. We were looking forward to it. It's a good thing my sister had the room because my parents, who live near her, were hosting a friend of the family who was traveling cross country. He is the son of my godparents, significant family friends whose initial acquaintance dates back to my father's early graduate school days in Texas. The son was designated female at birth, but transitioned in his young adult years. As small children, he and his sister participated in my wedding. I've since spoken with him on the phone, and he's just as kind and wonderful as I remembered.

Anticipating the taxing day of driving the next day through the Richmond-Washington-Baltimore corridor on Interstate 95 that is every traveler's nightmare, I went to bed early. Normally I leave my phone downstairs at night, but since I was traveling, I decided to keep my essential belongings in one place. Not quite ready to fall asleep, I scrolled through my phone and remembered my mother's email. Big mistake. The link in the email directed me to the American Thinker website. Because I'd never heard of the media outlet, I went straight to AllSides and found what I was dreading—it is a far-right publication. I won't even deign to call it "news." I immediately checked to see who the other recipients on this email chain were. And my heart sank because of one person in particular—my godfather.

I didn't know what was worse, the article or the source from which it came. American Thinker is a daily internet publication that touts interest in all topics relating to American politics, especially national security. Pop-up advertisements and irregular website formatting suggest funds are limited and in-house web support questionable. The website includes a list of staff with biographies, adding to an air of credibility, at least on the surface. But what caught my attention were its sources. According to the American Thinker website, "Contributors are accomplished in fields beyond journalism and animated to write for the general public out of concern for the complex and morally significant questions on the national agenda."[1] If I'm reading between the lines correctly, any lay person from any background with zero training or education in American politics or national security—never mind actual journalistic ethics and best practices—can submit an article for the public's consumption and dissemination. For some reason the proverbial eccentric uncle and wackadoodle neighbor across the street came to mind.

Then came the article itself, which introduces the National Parents and Families Engagement Council (NPFEC), newly created by the U.S. Department of Education "to facilitate strong and effective relationships between schools and parents, families and caregivers" by providing academic and mental support.[2] By the second paragraph, the argument begins to gain some heat when the author lists all of his grievances with the "elitist, left-wing" members of the council's advisory board with blurbs about their purported (and clandestine) LGBTQ+ and abortion agendas.[3] The author later ratchets up his disdain and calls them "communist-inspired organizations."[4] I visited the website of each council organization mentioned in the article and couldn't find any information corroborating his claims, and he included no sources to validate them in the article itself. From there the author takes us down our first rabbit hole to Vladimir Lenin, followed by the Marxist Frankfurt School, a short tour of the Vietnam War, and a litany of grievances about the alleged corruption of our universities by "woke" professors.

1. American Thinker, "About Us," lines 2–4.
2. U.S. Department of Education, "U.S. Department of Education Creates," lines 1–2.
3. Stansbury, "Biden Sets His Sights on K–12 Education," lines 8–28.
4. Stansbury, "Biden Sets His Sights on K–12 Education," lines 32.

Mind you, this crash course tracing the degradation of our education system happens in a single paragraph. Finally, he concludes his diatribe by providing two proposals to protect our kindergartners: support legislation "to constrain the enablers of the gender-transition fad" and "reintroduce civics to replace the divisive CRT indoctrination."[5]

Are you kidding me? *This* is what my mother sent?

I can imagine that the alleged LGBTQ+ "indoctrination" in our school systems, purported by the article, terrifies my mother. I would be terrified, too, if I believed the author's argument, and I'm sure that's why she sent it. To my mind, what's actually happening in our classrooms is something else entirely. It's not ominous and more about representation than anything else. For example, is it indoctrination when a teacher reads a story about a boy with two moms, especially when she knows two of her students have gay parents? Where is the threat in acknowledging the reality of her students' lives? Are people worried that simply hearing this story will suddenly "turn" children gay? Do children turn into a butterfly after reading *The Hungry Caterpillar*? No. Kids aren't concerned about who has two moms or two dads. What they want to know is if the boy in the story is happy and loved. That's what kids care about. My mother would argue that elementary students are too young to hear about homosexuality. I'd argue they're too young to understand conservative religious arguments against it. But one thing I know for sure: no child is too young to learn to show respect and kindness toward families—and people in general—who are different from theirs. The only way to teach children such lessons is if they see and hear and talk about them in a safe environment such as the classroom. Inclusive curricula help children, especially when they see themselves or their family systems represented in a loving and healthy framework. It's a proven fact that LGBTQ+ children perform better when they feel heard and valued for who they are.[6] We all do.

Miraculously, even after rereading the article my mother had sent in that email several times that first night at my sister's house, I still managed to fall asleep. Exhaustion from driving hours in traffic has that effect. What I couldn't do, however, was stay asleep. My spirit was too unsettled. In the early morning hours, I unplugged my phone, pulled up my notes app and began drafting a response with both thumbs. In spite of my lack of sleep, I was able to assemble my thoughts with extreme clarity in about

5. Stansbury, "Biden Sets His Sights on K–12 Education," lines 62, 68.
6. Bittker, "LGBTQ-Inclusive Curriculum," lines 30–33.

fifteen minutes. I showed great restraint by removing all negative words and anything connoting finger-pointing before I pressed "send." I offered suggestions and not just concern. And finally, I provided a reasonable call to action. I checked my spelling and punctuation, and, at the break of dawn, copied my response from my notes app to an email, but instead of just acknowledging my parents, I addressed each person on the initial email thread by name, and then I sent it:

> While I know many of you on this thread, please allow me to introduce myself to the rest of you. My name is Danielle Hensley, and I am the youngest daughter of Nate and Jean Alexander.
>
> Education is near and dear to my heart because I am a former high school English teacher myself, and both of my children are products of public school education.
>
> After reading this article, I came away with several insights that I'd like to share with you. I hope that you will humor me and read along to the end.
>
> One of the things I taught my students is about checking sources. It requires a bit of extra work, but in the end, it makes you a stronger learner and a more informed citizen. One of the sources to help us navigate the digital world is Allsides. While it's not perfect, it does provide a resource for helping us identify news biases.
>
> This article takes an obvious hard right stance when it equates liberals as communists and transgender issues as a fad. Is the article helpful in informing us? Perhaps. But I'd argue its main intent is for stoking fear.
>
> Fear is the weapon used throughout history to pit citizen against citizen. It's the main tactic of propaganda and a tool for dehumanization. And it's working, as evidenced in this article.
>
> How much stronger as a nation could we be if we all acknowledged these tactics, identify them when we see them, name them out loud, and refute their presence by not forwarding? And how much stronger could we be as a nation when we stay away from filling our minds with far right and far left news? Be intentional about what you feed your brain.
>
> Do you know anyone who is gay? How about someone who is transgender?
>
> I do.

Because I love them, I could never forward this article because doing so only foments the hatred against them. We are talking about
real people here, not abstract ideas.

Yes, we should stay abreast of what's happening in our schools and
government. But we also need to check ourselves when we enter
the conversation. And one way I like to do that is by asking myself,
"Who is my neighbor?"

Let's start reaping kindness and love, and kick hatred to the curb.
Our society will be better for it, and so will you.

I didn't know half of the people included on my mother's initial recipi-
ent list. Some of the names were familiar because my parents mention them
often in conversation, as if they are somehow my friends too. My sister was
on the list, as was my dad's best friend from his fraternity days, and I believe
I recognized their neighbor across the street as well. I wasn't sure how my
mother would feel about me essentially calling her out in public, but this
time I had to respond to the group because my godfather, the one whose
son is transgender, was also among the recipients. My parents were currently
hosting my godfather's transgender son, whom they will tell you they love,
while simultaneously spreading homophobic hate-filled rhetoric and fear-
mongering propaganda into the public square ad nauseam.

When teaching at Trinity, I often had to get creative with handouts
because, even in a private school setting, resources were limited. While my
students had access to an enormous literary anthology, that book largely remained on the shelf, not only because of its size but also because it glossed
over the meaty literary works I wanted my students to read. Needing a story
my students didn't have, I quickly found one online, and hastily printed out
a packet for each of them. With only a few minutes left in class, students
began reading it silently, and then came the sneers and the giggles. I even
had one student return her packet because she couldn't read it any more. I
asked her to show me why and when she did, I just about fainted. Despite
being referred to commonly as the "father of English literature," and despite
his fourteenth-century sensibilities, Geoffrey Chaucer can be rather raunchy,

depending on the translation. I quickly gathered up each packet and counted to make sure I had them all. I couldn't even bring myself to recycle the papers at school, so instead I brought them home.

I also used the experience as a real-life teachable moment for my students: I, their teacher, made a mistake by not reading the entire piece to make an informed decision about its appropriateness. If my mother sent the article without reading all of it, then we could also argue she might not agree with all of its hatred. Much like my Chaucerian *faux pas*, had she known, she wouldn't have forwarded it. What I wouldn't accept, however, is my sister wanting to give my parents a pass because of their age. Yes, they are older, but they're not senile. They still live independently. They still drive. My mother still preaches from the pulpit. They still vote. And they also still hit the send button on their computer.

To add more absurdity to this increasingly woebegone weekend, I'm almost positive my parents read my response before they arrived at my daughter's lacrosse game that morning. My dad is always the first one up, and his usual habits include sitting in his green leather recliner by the window with a cup of coffee while flipping open his laptop to check email or do word puzzles such as Quordle (Wordle's more difficult cousin). My email would have been waiting for him. Yet they said nothing at all about it at the game. If they hadn't read it before the match that morning, they certainly would have read it upon returning home after the tournament. But when we reconvened for dinner at my sister's house later that evening, they didn't mention, hint, or acknowledge anything about my electronic missive. Again, all I got was their silence and business as usual. Strangely, though, this time their silence actually did speak volumes to me. Their avoidance summed up the depth of dysfunction of our family system in real time. Instead of saying, "I read your email and need some time to respond," or, "You gave me a lot to think about," or even, "I'm mad as hell and can't talk about it right now," their silence made me and my feelings feel inconsequential—not even worth a response—while we wordlessly navigated around the 15,000-pound elephant sprawled on the living room floor.

In spite of my parents' radio silence, I did receive a few responses from other recipients. My sister's response was the first. She endorsed my comments wholeheartedly to the group, adding a reminder for folks that we should "love our neighbors as ourselves." This first act of outward solidarity by my sister felt nice and affirming. I also got a personal response from my godfather simply saying, "Thank you Danielle, my sweetheart."

My godfather, cut from the same swath as my dad, is highly educated and well-traveled, kind, and loving. He is a retired physician and an active bird-watcher. Yet, for reasons unknown to me, just like my father, he endorses Trump. He and my father regularly speak by phone, and have traveled together on bird-watching expeditions. My godfather even came to visit us when we lived in Panama so he could check the illusive and brightly colored Quetzal off his list. His wife, like me with my father, is consternated and dismayed by her husband's politics. After she reached out to me saying as much, we have been a support to one another throughout the 2020 election and beyond. She is the first person I called when my daughter formally identified as gay. And her spiritual gifts of gentleness and deep listening are exactly what I have needed. I wonder how my godfather reconciles my mother's beliefs as demonstrated by the article she shared with her hospitality toward his son. The emotional whiplash must be confusing. I wonder if he reached out to her to discuss what had transpired. More importantly, I wonder if my mother apologized to him. I don't know.

The most revealing response came from my dad's best friend from his undergraduate days at the University of Delaware. My dad particularly enjoys attending the university's sporting events and reunion weekends with him, evident in the numerous texts relaying the final score with attached pictures of the two of them in the bleachers. This man is the closest link my dad has to his college days, and my guess is their friendship makes my dad feel young. Shared memories of college experiences such as their fraternity house and locker room antics transport him nostalgically to his glory days. While I neither needed nor expected my father to come to my defense, his silence has let his college friend do all the talking for him. In much the same way as the author of the American Thinker piece, my dad's college friend's logic meandered from CRT to transgender issues to indoctrination of kindergartners to media biases by dropping bombshell accusations without any proof or explanation. And because, as he is quick to mention, he has had a gay, Black business partner for more than twenty years, he can't possibly be homophobic or racist, right? He doesn't have a problem with transgender people except when they ask for equality. And then there's Hunter Biden's laptop that, without a doubt, helped steal the 2020 election for Biden. He went on to list all of the corrupt Democratic mayors and district attorneys across the country. He is also part of the same frat group staunchly convinced that fellow alum Joe Biden, who "stands in front of the camera and blatantly lies," is unfit to serve. Even though their paths haven't crossed in probably a half century, this guy knows with absolute certainty that "[Biden] hasn't changed."

Because my parents said nothing to me directly before my daughter and I returned home from the tournament, I asked my sister to intervene on my behalf. Four days later my mother finally responded to me. She thanked me for my thoughtful response, yet still didn't seem to grasp the severity of what transpired. She implied she had done nothing wrong because her intent was simply to point out what was happening in our classrooms—doing her civic duty by informing us of the educational corruption of our youth by woke liberals. There was no contrition for the name-calling within the article, or how it may have hurt others who read it—including my godfather. No shame, embarrassment, or conviction (in the Baptist sense of that word). Certainly, she felt no compunction to ask for forgiveness. I knew my mother still didn't get it when she said in her email response to me that "love and truth go together." When I read those words, I lost it all over again.

During my sister's intervention, she discovered my mother had in fact read the whole article before she shared it, so our hypotheses fell apart as well as our hopes that this was just an innocent mistake. In light of this, my mom's ambivalence makes sense now. As was my typical response, I immediately rolled up my sleeves and set to work generating yet another email to her. I thoughtfully mapped out everything that was wrong with the American Thinker piece she'd shared. I was pulling out all the stops, showing her where the flaws existed in the author's argument, his use of propaganda techniques such as dehumanizing hate speech, and even his persuasive style of writing. I was about three pages in, typing feverishly and checking sources with multiple browsers open. Then, like a car running out of gas, I just quit.

My mind and spirit exhausted. I didn't feel anger or hatred or sadness. Just empty. And I knew I couldn't do it anymore. For the first time, I saw the absolute futility of trying to change my parents' thinking. All of this effort of time and mental energy for what? My parents are never going to believe me when I tell them the whole CRT-public-school-curriculum-thing is a made-up boogie monster perpetuated by Fox News. No, they aren't interested. They are in too deep.

Instead, I closed up my didactic email, and for the last time, laid it all out on the table:

Thank you for acknowledging my email. You say "love and truth go together." I couldn't agree more. And that's why you forwarding that article is so perplexing and alarming to me. The article reflects neither love nor truth, but instead foments hate and fear.

I'm happy to go through the article with you and show where, in my opinion, it misses the mark. However, for me there is a much larger issue. I don't know who you are any more. The mother of my youth would never have sent this article to anyone because her critical lens and moral compass would have guided her. The name calling and dehumanizing rhetoric would have stopped her in her tracks. And the lack of both sound facts and a logical argument would have raised her suspicions enough to throw it in the trash.

I have been begging you and Dad to take a critical look at the literature you consume. I've provided suggestions, including All-Sides on two separate occasions: Aug. 2020 and again in Jan. 2021. I even asked the following questions:

Would you be willing, alongside me, to modify your news absorption with intentionality? Unsubscribe from far-right media and strive to read, watch, and listen to middle of the road?

Neither of you responded.

I don't know how to help you. And perhaps you don't want any help. And that's okay. But I will not stay silent when anyone tries to marginalize a fellow human being.

I know my mom wants desperately to stay in relationship. And I think she was starting to understand the severity of her actions and how hurtful they were. I really want to believe that she doesn't think that way, but it's hard to reconcile when I look at the bigger picture of past conversations strung together. I wish I could say that my parents simply lost their way in 2016—a momentary lapse in judgment causing them to veer slightly off course. But deep down I know that's not true. I'm angry that my parents believe the things they do, yet all of that is wrapped up in their histories, which began long before I arrived. What gravely disappoints me is their complacency in challenging the beliefs they've clung to for far too long. They're content in repeating what they've heard on the news, recycling old tropes, and implicitly trusting their longtime friends to share only what is true—a trust that does not, it would seem, extend to their youngest child.

My parents remain perfectly comfortable with their silent resolve and a refusal to make waves. Challenging any of this takes a desire to learn and deconstruct. That is exhausting. And scary. They seem satisfied with saying, "I'm old—too old to change, grow, or evolve—and my fire is nearly extinguished." What's the point of attempting the impossible?

13

Building Bridges or Burning Them?

> We change the future by changing the way people think.... We change the way people think by changing the way we talk about things. To that end, I have encouraged people to speak up about what they think is important, to take up oxygen that otherwise feeds the hatred and division that have had far too much influence in our country of late.
>
> —Heather Cox Richardson

> I think there's a point in your healing journey where you stop trying to convince other people to do the right thing, you just observe their choices, understand their character, and decide what you're going to allow in your life.
>
> —Brianna Wiest

Each time I've started a new job, my employer has required some sort of personality assessment as part of the onboarding process to "promote intra-departmental success." While many people find them loathsome, such assessments amuse me and I anticipate the results as much as I might the prize at the bottom of the Cracker Jack box.

For my Introduction to Psychology class at Wheaton, we took the Myers-Briggs test. I felt the test was pretty accurate with my final "score" of I-N-T-J. When I started at Versado Training, the DiSC personality assessment confirmed that I am a Hard C—cautious, careful, and conscientious.

I think that's pretty accurate, too. The older I get, the more introverted and less flexible I become. Not surprisingly, I'm a "rules follower" who thrives on structure and order. Unforeseen change really irks me.

I found such personality testing especially helpful when I decided to switch careers in 2015. After we moved from Alexandria, Virginia, to North Carolina in 2011, I had difficulty finding a teaching job in the private sector. As a result, I decided to enroll in the lateral entry program at North Carolina State University, a two-year licensure program that provides the necessary skills to teach in a public school system. Once students in the program have completed enough credits, the state allows them to seek employment in the same pool as all the other licensed teachers. The competition was stiff. Even with my years of teaching in private schools, I realized quite early in the process that English teachers were a dime a dozen. Therefore, this employment process wasn't going to be easy.

After near defeat and a load of self-doubt, I eventually got a part-time job offer teaching two sections of high school freshman English. I was shocked because an initial phone conversation early in the process had gone horribly wrong, but in spite of that, the school district called me back a week later to schedule an in-person interview. In hindsight, I should have known they were desperate. Then again, so was I. The school was located almost an hour away from our home, so I spent nearly as much time in the car as I did in my classroom. Still, I was committed to making it work in addition to taking all the remaining night classes to complete my official certification and licensure.

Even though I had taught the same literature in years past, I was grossly ill-equipped to work in this public school setting. For starters, I wasn't prepared to work with students who weren't motivated to learn. Most students in my classes had behavioral issues; a third of them had an Individualized Education Program—a legal document under U.S. law that is developed for each public school child who needs special education nationwide. One such student was manic and often refused to take his medication. Another had just been released from juvenile detention. I was warned not to make yet another student angry because he might hit me. Some days I didn't have enough desks or textbooks for all my students. And a good day meant I didn't have to call security or the office for backup. I was paid to teach the state-mandated curriculum, but I had no idea how to reach my students. They didn't need poetry explications and Shakespeare; they needed bear hugs and unconditional love.

After a student threw a pen at me so hard that it ricocheted off the white board behind me and broke into several pieces, after only five months on the job, I knew I was done. (My hair falling out in the shower was another good indication that I was not the right person for this job.) Yes, it was only a pen, but the violent nature of the act is what got to me. A child tried to hit me. I went home, typed my letter of resignation, and emailed it immediately to my principal. When I returned the next day to gather my belongings and get materials ready for the substitute, a fellow teacher across the hall saw me making copies and told me that, for what it was worth, the administration had set me up for failure. I guess there was some consolation in hearing that, but deep down, on so many levels, I still felt like a failure. Quitting this teaching position meant the end of my enrollment in the licensure program, but more significantly, it drove the final nail in the coffin of my teaching career.

That final classroom experience was traumatic, and for months I replayed many of its scenes in my head in the attempt to make sense of them. After some time and healing, I did what I normally do—I started researching next steps. But I knew I needed help because I wasn't sure how to match my skills, personality, and any newfangled careers out there since the ubiquity of digital technology and so-called smart phones. A career change at my age was either risky or stupid, but with some life left in me, I decided to take a chance.

How would I narrow down so many options to a good vocational fit that complimented what I'd already accomplished? I needed this career change to make sense, like a gentle stretch to the next stepping stone rather than a clumsy quantum leap into the abyss.

I hate the adage "The world is your oyster." What a load of crap! I might have all the desire in the world to become an astronaut so I can float in outer space, but without the aptitude for math and science, it is never going to happen. Instead of telling impressionable students that they can do anything they set their mind to, I wish someone had told me early on to discover my passion and then fine-tune my vocational search to feed it. I've told both of my children to take as many different electives in high school as possible because you never know when that one art or music class might spark a life-long passion (or at least the road to it). So far, my theory has worked for my son. After taking a television/broadcasting elective and running his high school's morning news program, in college he is now a double major in film/media studies and government. That makes me proud of him, as well as very hopeful for him.

In the spirit of getting-it-right-the-next-time-around, I decided to work with a career counselor, someone trained to gather all the facets of my personality combined with my natural abilities to produce a list of careers out there that suit me best. After a couple weeks completing various computer modules, which were actually quite fun and felt like timed computer games, I received a glorious printout of the various vocations matching my skills. Not surprisingly, teacher was on the list. Don't get me wrong, I loved teaching. But the thought of teaching *Romeo and Juliet* for twenty additional years made me depressed because there are only so many ways to reinvent the wheel. Lawyer was also on the list, which made me laugh out loud. According to my career counselor, my results indicated the key ingredient to finding the next fulfilling career path was to make sure it's creative. I took her suggestion to heart and went all in by enrolling in graphic design at our local community college.

After two and a half years of learning Adobe's Creative Cloud design software—very much like learning a foreign language—I'm now creating graphics for a local nonprofit. Then came a new personality test. With this job, I discovered I'm a solid "gold" in the True Colors Personality Test: I respect rules and authority. I am also responsible, organized, appreciative—and here's the real kicker—loyalty driven.

Loyalty. That word struck me. I initially had to wrestle with it because two things immediately came to mind: a mafia boss and Donald Trump. Not coincidentally, Trump required loyalty repeatedly when referring to his inner White House circle, just like Don Corleone in *The Godfather*. Ironically, perhaps the need for loyalty is the only thing Trump and I have in common. But when I give that comparison further thought, Trump's need for loyalty is purely transactional—I'll scratch your back if you scratch mine—with little if any regard for the well-being of the other person. Trump's loyalty is a type of protection that insulates him from any accountability or consequences of his wrongdoing. So far, Trump's form of loyalty has been a very successful safety net for him.

I have the *Merriam-Webster Dictionary* app on my phone, largely because I'm a bad speller. I also use it as a quick reference to see if I'm using a particular word correctly, so I often find the usage examples are helpful as well. What really gets me excited is a word's history, etymology, and the century in which it was first used. The older the word, the more thrilling and weightier is becomes. As I scrolled through the app on my phone, the way I define loyalty for myself is far different than how Trump does, apparently. For me, loyalty isn't about obligation or blind fealty—it's all about the safety, comfort, and the stability of knowing who is on my side. For me, it's all about community, devotion, and commitment to a common core of ideals and shared beliefs—a mutual understanding. Loyalty is the glue that holds us together.

To fully understand the meaning of a word, it's also important to know its antonyms. Like that schmaltzy saying, "You can't appreciate the light until you've experienced darkness"—the same goes for looking at a word's opposite, for that's where nuance lives. Among the antonyms for loyalty, two hit me right between the eyes: inconstancy and infidelity.

Oh my God! That's it! Those two words are the gravitational pull helping me come to terms with why I've been so distraught with my family during Trump's term in office and beyond. I feel betrayed by my people—my own flesh and blood—when I needed them most.

I thought I knew "my people" and understood the mutually agreed-upon Christian values and social mores that guide our circle. My disillusionment is not because I feel we all must believe the same things—no, that's not it at all. Instead, when the "rules" were allowed to change without my receiving so much as a memo, it felt as if the rug had been pulled out from under me. I suppose the irony is that my sense of morality would never have allowed me to sympathize with Trump, never mind full-throatily endorse him, even if I had received such a rule-change memo.

Because part of my understanding of loyalty means an adherence to shared values, just like the "moral contract" from Trevor Noah's video, morality also has a large role in shaping who I am. Morality isn't a synonym to loyalty, but it is tangentially related for me because it's all about doing what is right. And, again, perhaps ironically, I credit my strong moral compass to my parents, who showed me what it means as a Christ-follower to live as an upright citizen and to love my neighbor.

Morality, however, may be the wrong word here because it's too gray. Perhaps a better word is Truth. It either is, or it isn't. When my son was about five years old, he asked me if Santa was real. I had a split second to decide how to answer because a long delay would breed suspicion. I stalled by asking him what he thought. I didn't have the heart to string him along so I could stretch out the days of his childhood for my selfish pleasure. He really wanted to know, and he trusted me to speak the truth. He was satisfied to learn that Santa of the red suit and reindeers is fake, but that Saint Nicholas was a real man. Some of the moms at our playgroup, however, were not so delighted at this revelation and politely reminded me to warn my son not to spill the beans about Santa vs. Saint Nick in front of their children.

When I asked my father how a practicing Christian could vote for Trump, I suspect it made him angry. It's the one question I'd been waiting for prominent evangelicals and moderate Republicans to ask out loud, but no one seemed willing. Somebody had to do it first, so I asked it myself. I know dad didn't appreciate me challenging his commitment to Christian virtue and his voting practices, but I'm sure there are dozens of times that same question crossed his mind when I voted for both Bill and Hillary Clinton and for Obama—twice. Without waiting for my father's response, I followed up my jarring question by providing my own answer: *Being a practicing Christian and voting for Trump are incompatible.* Gasp. I really said that. How audacious of me.

Without a doubt, my comments were aggressive, but I couldn't think of any other way to say it, especially when all my other methods to reach him fell flat. I wasn't trying to be snarky or judgmental. I was confronting him because I really needed to understand my father's thoughts on the matter. Like my son with Santa Claus, I needed to know the truth. The first time my father put a Republican presidential yard sign in the flower beds of his upper-middle-class Washington, DC, house, their friends and neighbors across the street casually said to his face that they were very surprised to learn his political leanings. One even said she thought he was smarter than voting for a Republican. To question my father's intelligence was just about as bad as me questioning his morality.

Fuming, my dad turned on his heels and forever held a grudge against the neighbor, even after her husband later apologized for her *faux pas.* That was also the last time my dad openly displayed his political party for all the world to see.

One of the last emails my brother-in-law sent during our political conversations included a pivotal statement. He made the argument that because we both voted in 2020 with our conscience, informed by our line in the sand, "no Christian can judge another Christian on the choice they made." I knew exactly the semantic trap being set—one gilded in Scripture and pointing straight to the jugular of Christian defense and criticism. *Judge not, lest ye be judged. Beware of casting the first stone. You didn't notice the log in your own eye? God is my judge, not you.* The finest examples of Christian moralism meant to stop accountability in its tracks. You can still be wrong even if you vote with your conscience, and yes, I can hold you accountable for that failure.

As Christians, maybe judgment is all we have left. If we all are fallible and our choices are too, maybe it's high time we start naming it. Out loud. The prophets of the Hebrew Scriptures did that naming and warned against worshiping idols, just like the literal golden Trump idol presented to the conservative audience at the 2021 Conservative Political Action Coalition (CPAC), the largest and most influential gathering of conservatives in the world:

> And Elijah came to all the people, and said, "How long will you falter between two opinions? If the LORD is God, follow Him; but if Baal, follow him." But the people answered him not a word.[1]

I'm no prophet. And the "judgment" I've presented to my family is not a "holier than thou attitude," at least that's a posture I've tried hard to avoid. Instead, it's an iron-sharpens-iron effort, a calling out—not for censorship but for accountability. Just like Mordecai had to remind Queen Esther of their shared Jewish heritage so that she might save their people from genocide at the hands of her husband, the Persian King Xerxes (Esther 4:12–14), I, too, am trying to remind my family of who they are and to whom we belong—a God of unconditional love, and not a God of condemnation. Because I love my family, we must talk about all of it—the blessings and the curses. "Not my job," you say? Who, then, is my neighbor? Because being a Christ-bearer means being a Truth-teller. My criticism of my family members' votes is not unpatriotic and disloyal. In fact, it's just the opposite.

When I step back and look at the bigger picture of my family, I was trying to save them. While my actions were driven by the best of intentions, I see now how my methods were not always the healthiest or most productive. But it was the best I could do amid the fear and panic about my family members standing on the wrong side of history.

I was desperate. Whether they wanted it or not, I was fighting for them with all my being, so that together we could be on the side of Power With. Of decency, empathy, love. But I'd missed that memo about Christians turning our moral filter on and off like a light switch (complete with dimmer function) whenever the need arose. Moving the moral goal posts—or in my brother-in-law's case, removing it altogether—to

---

1. 1 Kgs 18:21.

accommodate political views is a dangerous game that damages, if not destroys, any Christian witness. And it's created an ever-widening separation within my family that I do not know how to reconcile.

During my parents' most recent visit to attend the wedding of another of our cousins, I overheard my father and my husband talking in the kitchen. Dad was all ruffled about the news surrounding Hunter Biden's laptop. With a raised voice, he proclaimed that *the American people deserve to know the truth!* I'm glad to hear that truth still matters to him. But I wish that same fervor and quest to know the truth also applied to Russia's involvement in our elections, Trump's two impeachments, the seven hours of missing presidential phone logs from the January 6 Capitol riot, and all those TOP SECRET and highly classified files discovered strewn about Mar-a-Lago in August 2022. Sadly, the fact that, in my father's mind, Hunter Biden's laptop takes precedence over Trump's dereliction of duty and potentially illegal actions that may have jeopardized our national security tells me he still is watching and listening to right-wing voices.

So, imagine my surprise when I learned my parents eventually did have a change of heart about Trump. A mutual friend relayed the news to me during a phone call. At first, I was elated, but then I felt the knife turn. My parents didn't owe me anything, but that they hadn't told me directly made me sad and angry. What had been the final straw for them? I've tossed that question around quite a bit, conjecturing that what happened at the Capitol must have prompted my parents' quiet exit out the back door. Maybe Trump's encouraging hordes of his supporters to storm the Capitol so he could reclaim his "rightful seat" had left them, like it had left me and countless others around the globe, aghast. Then there were the chants of "Hang Mike Pence!" Maybe that did it.

Whatever the catalyst or final straw was for them, why hadn't they bothered to tell me? After all my efforts to convince them about Trump, they knew such a sea change would have been important to me. Were they ashamed about their lack of good judgment? Were they afraid their revelation might be met by my righteous indignation and a chorus of "I told you so?" My husband told me later that my dad also confessed in the kitchen the day of that wedding that he couldn't talk to me about politics because I don't listen.

While stinging, my father's accusation contains kernels of truth. I listen, but I'm not easily convinced. I now engage in political conversations and don't shy away from them. A new and, to some people, including my father, apparently, unrecognizable part of me has evolved and emerged. I'm opinionated, but now I am also informed. Perhaps that's what riled my dad most. He didn't like what I had to say and the conviction with which I said it. I'm direct, and that is off-putting. No kid gloves.

For four years during Trump's disastrous administration, I was in fight-or-flight mode with my hair on fire, trying to find my footing, to reconcile all the incongruous parts of my upbringing with a family that accepted a president who unapologetically normalized the worst of humanity. I was paying close attention to my family's every word and gesture, all their spoken and unspoken communications. And I did not like what I heard (nor what I didn't hear). But I also didn't know how to debate with my father when he championed biased news and seemed ambivalent about adopting a more complete set of facts. In that sense, I was listening, but yes, I was unwilling to entertain his inanities.

I'm glad my parents no longer support Trump. There is relief in that knowledge, but it sadly didn't magically make it all better. Some days it feels as if the very fabric holding my family of origin together is disintegrating from dry rot. I've squeezed out all my vulnerability and laid bare the attempts and failures of my political and moral awakening. I have exposed my deepest pains—a colossal risk—in the hope of fostering an ever-more authentic connection with people I love.

In hindsight, perhaps I might have had better results if I had repackaged my pain in a way that made them feel less uncomfortable. But where is the honesty in that? I've cried and screamed and pleaded—not to shame them, but because my body (and soul) knew no other recourse.

It has taken me years, but I've finally been able to pinpoint the source of my profound anger. It's not simply that my family of origin and I don't agree about presidents, politics, or abortion. Neither is it simply because the lenses through which we view Scripture are different shades and prescriptions. No. My anger is about not being heard, and at the root of that anger is a fear of being ostracized and ignored.

It's such a simple thing when you stop and think about it. Hearing and seeing someone. It's the most basic form of human decency because it validates that that person exists and has worth. We may not agree, but I still see you. And I respect you enough to want to listen to what you have to say, no matter how you say it, and no matter how hard it might be to hear—because we are family, and families love unconditionally.

The flip side of not being seen and heard is being shunned, an intentional practice that says only certain parts of your story, or God forbid none of it at all, are worthy of attention. To ignore me is the ultimate act of denying my inherent value as a child of God, not to mention their beloved child.

I appreciate that my dad made the conscious effort in his parenting not to repeat the kind of verbally abusive behavior that he experienced during his own childhood. He broke that cycle, and I am eternally grateful. But his silence toward me is now the thorn in my flesh. Ultimately, it shows cowardice and selfishness, as well as a piece of my late grandmother's vindictiveness when he is willing to talk about these issues with others—and sometimes just within earshot—but never directly with me.

Silence protects him, and it deprives me of closure. But I get it. It's easier to "cancel" me than to reopen old wounds, or to stand up and take even one shred of responsibility for his actions and complicity in the shattering of our family system. Remaining silent builds walls with sharp corners. It may be (and I sincerely hope that it is) a temporary coping mechanism, but it fails to heal any hearts. I've tried to break this pattern. But it takes two to have a conversation.

I failed miserably in my attempt to reach my parents. And oh, how I wish they would be brave enough to enter this vulnerable and important conversation. I wanted them to fight like hell on my behalf until we could come to some understanding because they know I'm worth it, that our relationship is worth it, because I am their precious daughter, and they love me unconditionally. I've tried to find an analogy that they might understand, one that accurately portrays my utter confusion around the Christian values of my youth—kindness, equity, morality, truth—and the dissonance with parents and other family members who supported, excused, and voted for Trump, many of them twice. It's something like a nurturing and devoted father who throws an elaborate wedding for his daughter. The only problem is the daughter is marrying a known abuser. The story will never have a happy ending.

My anger came from a real place of fear. And I think my parents knew this but didn't want to dig any deeper, knowing it had the potential to implicate them. My dad has an answer for just about everything—from broken-down cars to proofing bread yeast—as if he holds all the secrets of life. And for much of my life, I believed every word. I trusted him unwaveringly. Why wouldn't I? And he even wore military fatigues pressed with so much starch and heat the pleats stood at attention to prove it. For his little girl, Dad personified safety and everything that was right in the world.

Have my parents heard anything I've said? I don't know. And at this point, does it really matter? Hasn't the damage already been done?

My husband assures me that I've done my level best to build bridges to connect with my family. But unless they are willing to walk across them, or at the very least meet me halfway, then the bridges are essentially useless. Still, I refuse to pull them down. The bridges remain intact should any of them have a change of heart.

But what am I supposed to do in the meantime?

14

What If I'm Wrong?

No one changes unless they want to. Not if you beg them. Not if you shame them. Not if you use reason, emotion, or tough love. There's only one thing that makes someone change: their own realization that they need to do it.

—Lori Deschene @3amthoughts

We cannot position ourselves in the middle when issues of justice and the well-being of our neighbors are involved. Justice takes sides.

—Jemar Tisby @jemartisby

When President Biden addressed the nation at Independence Hall in Philadelphia on September 1, 2022, I did not watch it. Instead, I was participating in The Great Troublemaker Turnout, an online meeting with more than five thousand women from throughout the United States that, unfortunately, overlapped with the president's last-minute scheduled speech.

The topic of the Zoom Troublemakers' meeting was about voting, voting rights, and what we can do in our family and friendship circles to make sure people get to the polls and vote Democratic. More importantly, the keynote speaker was Heather Cox Richardson, and I really wanted to hear what she had to say. I also didn't feel compelled to watch Biden's speech because he isn't the best public speaker. Yes, I know he works incredibly hard at public speaking to compensate for his life-long speech impediment. But the more he stutters, the more fodder Republicans have to make their spurious claims of incapacity in general and dementia in particular, and I just didn't have the energy to hold my breath for the duration of his oration, no matter how kind he may be.

I didn't watch or listen, but I did read Biden's speech. "Remarks by President Biden on the Continued Battle for the Soul of the Nation" was great because of two opposing things: on the one hand, he sought to draw us together as a nation and, on the other, he separated the chaff from the wheat when he named the greatest present threat dividing our democracy. Biden reminded us that we have endured much as a young nation largely because of our collective regard for "We, the People." We value liberty and freedom, but we cannot take those pillars for granted.

And then Biden quickly named names. He did so formally and with all the authority of the presidential seal that adorned the podium from which he spoke and the American flags that flanked him. He said it out loud. Biden not only put Donald Trump and the MAGA Republicans together in the same sentence, he also named their agenda as "an extremism that threatens the very foundations of our republic."[1]

Finally. And thank God! But as relieved as I was to hear the president say the hard thing, I also knew it was probably a little too late. Did the half of our nation that voted for Trump in 2020—those folks who needed to hear it most—listen at all? Because Fox News didn't air Biden's live prime-time speech, my guess is no. Then did my family at least read what Biden had to say if they didn't listen or watch him deliver his speech? Did they let his words sink in? I just don't know.

I'm either a slow learner, an eternal optimist, or a glutton for punishment. Probably a little of all three. I grew up with the adage: you can't change other people; you can only change yourself. I know this rule. So, why on earth did I try so hard, only to arrive at the same conclusion that I cannot, in fact, change my family even though, Lord knows, I have tried? All of my attempts to reach them—the articles, emails, book buying, letters, texts, instant messages, and face-to-face conservations—have any of these efforts moved their needle *any* closer to the middle? Not by any evidence I've seen. If anything, my endeavors have only made them dig their heels in deeper. Hence, the silent treatment.

In the end, nothing will change for my family members unless they want it to. They must decide to ask the uncomfortable questions, and be at

1. White House, "Remarks by President Biden," lines 31–32.

peace with uncertainty. Jesus himself asked a lot more questions than he answered, so "maybe faith isn't about certainty, but learning to ask—and sit in the complexity of—good questions."[2] But if and when they reach the point that they see their long-held beliefs no longer hold water, yet they insist on finding answers, maybe it's time to search outside of their religious and political echo chambers, and to adjust their opinions. Ultimately, they have to decide if, when, and how to deconstruct. It is a process that requires intellectual humility and a self-awareness that demands they admit they do not, in fact, have all the answers—and to be at peace with this uncertainty. But unfortunately, that is not the language of most conservative Christians. The historian and *New York Times* bestselling author Jemar Tisby, PhD, said it so plainly when he relayed a non-Christian's generalization about evangelicals as "people who don't have any questions."[3] Change requires the curiosity (and bravery) to ask one of the most vulnerable questions I know: *What if I'm wrong?*

There is nothing I can do or say that will move my family closer toward this introspective process. The choice is entirely and unequivocally theirs.

But there is one person in my family who is actively working toward a greater understanding—my sister. Although she has said very little to me about her DEI training, which I find both curious and sad—about what new things she's learned or any old beliefs she's thrown away—I do know she feels passionately about what it means to "love thy neighbor." It is in this vein that she seeks to reshape the demographics of her largely White, heterosexual, middle-to-upper-class, nondenominational community Bible church. Church leaders did not ask her to take the course, nor was there any financial gain for her to do so. She took this step because she saw a need, an imbalance in her church, her job, and her community where equal representation of all God's children does not exist. And I whole-heartedly applaud her for that, especially when many members of her faith tradition and community scoff at the need for DEI education at all.

In her passion to make a difference in her house of worship, she sought out tools to help bridge this gap. And when she found her curriculum of choice, she called me with great relief and enthusiasm. She was so excited; I could feel her almost levitating through the phone line. She was sure this particular series would reshape her church and help it become more inclusive, more loving. I was excited for her, too, until I went to the

2. Nye, "In the gospels, Jesus is asked 187 questions," Twitter, June 19, 2022.
3. Tisby, "Someone who is not Christian," Instagram, September 14, 2022.

program's website and started poking around. When I googled "The Center for Faith, Sexuality & Gender," I quickly learned the organization is all about LGBTQ+ issues, but within a conservative "biblical" framework. I know the history between the LGBTQ+ community and conservative Christian theology is nothing shy of oil and water—the two don't mix. Will this organization, comprised of "Christian pastors, leaders and theologians who aspire to be the Church's most trusted source of theologically sound teaching" be any different?[4]

What got my immediate attention was on the organization's landing page. The "hook" inside a big blue text box with large font said: "Your biggest question. . . ." Then what proceeded was a very familiar sounding dilemma: "My lesbian daughter just got engaged, should I attend her wedding?" Holy cow! This is the same type of conundrum my father expressed out loud at the beach several years ago about whether he and my mother should attend the wedding of a friend's gay child. At the time, I was shocked that my father, a professed practicing Christian, was asking this type of question. I naively attributed his questioning to a generational gap, that my dad was just woefully out of touch. I am shocked now to know that this is a real thing—that fellow Christians have to click the "Explore" button at this website and spend money on Grace/Truth 1.0 and 2.0 to find out what Jesus would do. Has loving our neighbor really become this complicated?

Yet there had to be something more to this organization for my sister to be so excited by the possibilities as if she'd found a long-lost coin. What about this organization sets it apart from the others? Is there really something revolutionary here that can meaningfully change how conservative Christians relate to the LGBTQ+ community? I was hopeful. As I navigated deeper into the website, I listened to the CEO's video clip about its mission. On first pass, it sounded hopeful because he was saying all the right things about welcoming gays and lesbians as children of God who are worthy of our love. Now, I could understand why my sister was so enthusiastic. Finally, a conservative Christian organization that was actively and intentionally seeking to bring the LGBTQ+ community into a "safe and compassionate environment" when most churches have purposefully and successfully banished them from it.

But then what happens once you get homosexuals inside the church? That part wasn't as explicitly clear on their website. Perhaps if I had purchased their twelve-part video series for $49.00, I'd be better able to answer

4. Center for Faith, Sexuality & Gender, "What We Do," lines 3–6.

this question. But here's where the rubber meets the road. Once I clicked on their "Statement of Marriage, Sexuality & Gender" link, I knew what was really going on here. Statement #1 says: "While same-sex marriage is legal in some countries, it does not represent a historical, Christian view of marriage," followed by Statement #4: "Simply experiencing attraction to the same sex (or being gay) is not in itself a morally culpable sin." Under these beliefs, what's left for the homosexual? Celibacy? Is that it? As long as you don't act on your attraction with a same-sex person, you're safe. But as soon as you've crossed that line, you're doomed. But not to worry because Statement #3 says that because of The Fall "all people—straight or non-straight—experience corruption in their sexuality."[5] Is that statement meant to bring some relief?

This website told me everything I needed to know. It's the same old song and dance of *hate the sin, but love the sinner*. The only new method used by this organization is its desire to welcome gays and lesbians into the church community as a new mission field ripe for the picking. But once they're in the pews, the old rule still applies: practicing homosexuality, even if in a loving, legally married union, is a sin. It's like offering a gay person a seat at your finely appointed table only to serve him table scraps while the rest of the guests eat filet mignon. The only difference now, according to the CEO's welcome video, is that they're going to emulate how Jesus loved: They will "love them into the Truth" with a capital T. In other words, the gay teenager will be so drawn by this new radical form of "love" that he/she/they will be compelled to change his/her/their ways to fit into the organization's "Truth" of what marriage should look like.

Of course, loving gay people is a good thing, not just because loving them is a biblical mandate, but because it's plain human decency. Shouldn't we all be loving our fellow humans unconditionally and not wait for some organization to give us permission and instructions on how to do so? More importantly, what Christians tend to forget is that God's ultimate model of love found in John 3:16 ("For God so loved the world that he gave his only Son, so that everyone who believes in him may not perish but may have eternal life"), the same verse many new Christians commit to memory, also has a profound encore. But unfortunately, most Christians can't recite John 3:17. Jesus' own words remind his disciples that he did not come "into the world to condemn the world, but in order that the world might be saved through him." So as a Christian, how do you justify condemning my gay daughter in

---

5. Center for Faith, Sexuality & Gender, "Statement of Faith," lines 2–4, 9–10, 6–8.

the name of Jesus Christ, when Jesus himself did not come to condemn her? How exactly do you get that authority, and in who's name?

But there's another problem to my sister's new-found curriculum. And it's a doozy. While this organization's approach to reaching the LGBTQ+ community might be a revolutionary concept for my sister, it is a smack in the face of authentic DEI scholarship—in particular, the second "E" pillar that stands for equity. If equity, as part of the DEI philosophy, means being impartial and fair by "trying to understand and give people what they need to enjoy full, healthy lives,"[6] yet the church bars people from marrying those whom they love, then in fact, the church is doing the exact opposite. In other words, if the long-held conservative view that same-sex marriage is a sin, and the church won't marry a gay couple, then it is excluding a particular group from a sacramental rite available to almost all heterosexuals. (How individual congregations and denominations deal with divorced people and their "worthiness" for receiving such a sacrament vary.) Nothing about that is equitable or inclusive.

My sister, however, eventually will have to make a decision. Right now, her religious beliefs and her secular DEI training do not align because evangelicalism, at least in its current popularly understood American iteration, does not fully embrace equity and inclusivity. In theory? Only up to a certain point. But in practice? No way. One system contradicts the other. And so, my sister has two options: she can cast aside the DEI tenants or she can reevaluate her religious beliefs. Such a shift has the potential to upend everything she's ever been taught. For her to completely merge DEI ideals and the biblical mandate to unconditionally "love thy neighbor" equitably, she's going to have to go back to the beginning and see what other experts and religious scholars have to say about Jesus and homosexuality. In essence, my sister must set aside all conservative scholarship and theology, and open her heart and mind to listen to what other devout Christians and scholars have to say about homosexuality and Jesus' gospel of radical inclusivity. Even if she does consider counterarguments and broaden her definition of "Truth," it is still entirely possible that my sister will arrive at a different conclusion than mine.

The same method is required for my sister to understand the depth and breadth of systemic racism as it exists now and historically, as she claims to do, and not just name racism in the places that are easy to spot, but in every system of our society. She must stop reading the books on her

6. Annie E. Casey Foundation, *Race, Equity and Inclusion*, 5.

shelf written by conservative Christian luminaries such as Mark Driscoll, Tim LaHaye, and James Dobson with a "Christian" agenda that elevates, protects, and worships White, male dominance. She's also not going to find many answers in *Christianity Today*. Instead, she needs to turn to the Black and Hispanic voices of her children's birth parents, hear their stories and research their histories, then see if she can tell her biracial children that systemic racism is a myth.

I know all of this re-education and unlearning will be a herculean effort for her because her go-to response to conflict resolution is to find tools that fit neatly and comfortably within her theology without challenging it or pushing boundaries. Most of us are programmed from birth to insulate ourselves with the things that support our status quo and beliefs. That's when we feel safest. No matter how enlightened or woke we may be, each of us falls prey to the confirmation bias habit. But if my sister is interested in making herself vulnerable through deconstruction, she can start by asking herself whether the interpretations of the Bible that she was taught by her conservative church are consistent with Jesus' love hermeneutic. In Matthew 22:35–40, Jesus claimed that the whole law of Moses was summed up by the commands to love God (Deuteronomy 6:4–5) and to love your neighbor as yourself (Leviticus 19:18). He interpreted the whole law through that lens. This is why Saint Augustine could later write: "Whoever, then, thinks that he [sic] understands the Holy Scriptures, or any part of them, but puts such an interpretation upon them as does not tend to build up this twofold love of God and our neighbor, does not yet understand them as he ought" (Augustine, *On Christian Doctrine*, 1.36.40). So a good place for my sister to start would be to ask this question: Do the interpretations of Scripture my church teaches conform to the love that Jesus taught and modeled for us?

I hope she will. For her niece's sake.

> And no one puts new wine into old wineskins. For the wine would burst the wineskins, and the wine and the skins would both be lost. New wine calls for new wineskins. (Mark 2:22)

15

Rainbows and Unicorns

> One reason people resist change is because they focus on what they have to give up, instead of what they have to gain.
>
> —Rick Godwin @progressivechristianity

The bridges I've built feel useless because my family refuses to cross them. If my desire is to remain in meaningful fellowship with my family members, despite the failure of all of my attempts to reach them, what are my options?

I can't keep doing what I've been doing for the last several years because, as we know, one of the definitions of insanity is doing the same thing over and over again and expecting a different outcome. That's already proven fruitless. And maddening. With the 2022 midterms just weeks away as I write these words, panic is bubbling to the surface, and out of frustration and fear, I want to barrage my family with articles about the hundreds of GOP candidates on the ballot at all levels of government who are election deniers.

While I'm tempted to fall back into my old habits, I've showed great restraint by sending just one article to my sister about the dangers of voting for election deniers. I'm hopelessly hopeful she'll read it and take it seriously when she votes. But at the same time, I know trying to change my family members is a futile exercise that exhausts me and distances them. Sadly, there is no magic bullet or secret sauce. Perhaps insanity and hope are actually close cousins.

Another option would be to ignore our political and religious disparities altogether; in essence, to wave the White flag and adopt a don't-ask-don't-tell policy when it comes to politics and faith. Why can't we just all get along?

Sticking my head in the sand and keeping my mouth shut to maintain a veneer of happy coexistence is flat out wrong *for me*. It may keep the peace—*their peace*—but I can't live in some fairy-tale La-La Land where our conversations are reduced to rainbows and unicorns. I know of countless friends living this way with their conservative family members. They are willing to keep quiet and just move along, but they are not happy. Their family relationships are fractured and strained. And this is essentially what my family and I are doing presently. But it feels so inauthentic to me. The small talk is soul-killing. And then there is that damn elephant lying prostrate on the living room floor because he has grown so big, he no longer fits under the Thanksgiving table.

If I am going to live in a La-La Land of rainbows and unicorns, I need guardrails. For example, I'm happy to talk about the weather and share recipes—I will be kind toward you—but I'm not willing to sit with you in a church pew before Christmas dinner.

God, that sounds so conditional and unloving, I realize, but I've had to wrestle with this concept for a long time, so hear me out. The Republican party has shifted. When the Republican party has had years and so many opportunities to hold Trump accountable and publicly denounce him—and they've done nothing except to circle the wagons—I think it's pretty safe to say the old GOP is dead. Whether you like this shift or not, if you call yourself a Republican, the rest of America hears and sees MAGA. So if your politics still support this new Republican party of bad behavior—election denying and suppressing, promoting lies over truth, justifying or ignoring an insurrection, stripping constitutional rights away from many Americans, fraternizing with hate groups, elevating White nationalism, banning books, white-washing American history, and dehumanizing the LGBTQ+ community (along with the new target of drag queens)—all in the name of Jesus and saving unborn babies, I'm out.

Don't tell me "Jesus loves you," "I'll be praying for you," or other religious platitudes when your politics say the exact opposite. How can I listen to my mother's homilies with the dissonant clanging of "those mothers" and "transgenderism is a fad" still ringing unresolved in the background? It is not okay for me to put on temporary blinders so I can stay laser-focused on her sermon while she's in the pulpit and block out her peripheral hate speech when she's not. Even though I know her and love her fiercely, until my mother makes the choice for reconciliation and forgiveness to all offended, I cannot listen to her preaching the gospel because I know now that *justice requires I take a side.*

Maybe I take my line-in-the-sand one step further and a bit deeper, an idea I never considered until I first came across Ryan Short's story. Ryan Short, a middle-aged gay son, had a telephone conversation with his eighty-year-old father. The father, unprovoked during the course of their conversation, committed his allegiance to the GOP. Flustered, Short sent an email to the entire family where he laid out one decisive boundary: "Hear me clearly—you cannot vote for the GOP and continue to have a relationship with me. No exceptions."[1]

I hadn't really thought about what a boundary should or shouldn't look like. But Short's story really hit home for me in a way that helped me make sense of my own relationship with my family, particularly with my father. My father's silence toward me, I feel he believes, is his boundary. He desperately wants to maintain a relationship with me, so instead of addressing my difficult and often confrontational questions, emails, and texts, he ignores them. But a boundary is more than just a line in the sand. It's not just an Either/Or, or in his case, a silencing. The problem is my father has never verbalized to me the *why*, and because of that, his lack of an explanation allows my imagination to revisit some dark places of our past. Because he provides no *why*, I naturally fill in the gaps, and that's where the danger lies. Ambiguity becomes the dark monster in the night.

No, my father's "boundary"—his silence—is actually not a boundary at all but a withdrawing. Perhaps my political prodding is emotionally overwhelming for him, so instead of engaging on any level, he shuts down. I get that, since I can be very passionate about things important to me. Perhaps ignoring the difficult problem is my father's go-to coping mechanism, and thus his silence is a natural byproduct. According to Dr. Leah Katz, a clinical psychologist, author, and public speaker, "setting a boundary is clearly articulating what you need and how you're feeling about what is happening."[2] What my father has done is definitely not that.

---

1. Cohen and Zitser, "A Gay Man's Mass Email," lines 13–14.

2. Katz, "WITHDRAWING is not the same thing as SETTING A BOUNDARY," Instagram, May 5, 2023.

While I am not the gay child here, my daughter is, and the same feverish rage boils to the surface with the hypocrisy when my family continues to support the increasingly dehumanizing post-Trump Republican platform. Whether or not my family will admit it, if they continue to vote Republican, their vote says, *I love you, Claire, but because of my interpretation of Scripture, I don't agree with your "chosen" lifestyle.* And because of this justification, their Republican vote permits them to continue with, *I love you, Claire, but I'm going to punish your sinful lifestyle by voting with a party that is methodically and purposefully putting laws into place that will marginalize you.* How is any of this love, I ask?

I hope one day, when my daughter's sexual orientation no longer remains hidden, I will be able to quote Ryan Short with as much conviction and say to my family members, "To vote GOP is to divide the family"[3]— YOU CHOOSE. Lucky for Short, his father and nearly everyone in his extended family agreed and confirmed they will no longer vote for Republican candidates—they chose him.

Since grappling with these various options about how to move forward with my family, I've had to fine-tune my original question. It now goes like this: If my family is not willing to engage with me or work toward reconciliation, and I can't change the direction of my moral compass, what options do I have left? That's my million-dollar question.

My aunt Brenda, who, as a child, gave away her beloved doll collection because of my grandmother's insistence, still worships her even long after her death. In spite of enduring a lifetime of my grandmother's verbal and psychological abuse, and her incessant criticisms, Brenda rarely missed celebrating an Easter or Christmas with her parents. Even as a mother with her own family, Brenda always came home. Why? My guess is she came back hoping the next visit would be better, or the next holiday would be the one filled with kindness, gentleness, and love. Or, as the dutiful daughter, maybe Brenda didn't realize she even had a choice about whether or not to come home. Maybe she feared she'd be ridiculed all over again if she didn't come home often enough. Or maybe this was her only understanding of love, and so she took whatever scraps of affection she could get. As a grandmother now herself, Brenda's pain is still visible because when she frequently invokes my late grandmother's name, she does so longingly, as if somehow saying the word "mother" could resurrect something good from beyond the grave.

3. Cohen and Zitser, "A Gay Man's Mass Email," lines 21–22.

Is it always the child's responsibility to strive for peace and reconciliation? Like Brenda, am I supposed to keep coming back, hoping my family will finally take some ownership so we can move toward reconciliation? The same Jesus who blessed the peacemakers in the Beatitudes also flipped the tables of the money changers in the temple. At what point is enough, enough?

A final choice for me is to walk away. A formal separation or, to use my mother's suggestion, a divorce. When Jesus sent the twelve disciples out to spread the good news, first to their own people, the Jews, he gave them a warning. Jesus told them if the Jewish people of a given town weren't interested in hearing their message, they were to "dust off their sandals,"[4] a symbolic gesture "to be done with them," and move along to the next town where people might be more receptive. Perhaps that's what I'm supposed to do, too?

Today, my family of origin has chosen to dwell in the world of rainbows and unicorns—where our relationship is distant but manageable. We may never move from here. But to progress for my own mental health and growth, I can choose any one of the options I've previously laid out. And most importantly, I can learn to forgive. That's the one action I haven't mentioned because frankly, it sounds so cliché—like *deus ex machina* in a Greek tragedy that magically appears with ropes and pulleys to neatly tie up all the loose ends of the plot.

Forgiveness does not mean I forget. It does not mean I sweep my brokenness under the rug, then sprinkle it with God's grace like pixie dust to remove the pain. No, I don't have the luxury of forgetting because the politicians my family members vote into office are the same ones who seek systematically to strip rights away from my gay daughter. She is about to enter the adult world where hate speech has been normalized, and her rights as a woman and as a queer person are being stripped away by the Supreme Court piece by piece. I cannot forget.

Nor does forgiveness mean I make excuses for them. They are adults, and they can choose to unlearn and relearn. Just recently my parents mentioned using AllSides to help identify trustworthy news sites. I'm beyond thrilled they've added this tool to their critical thinking arsenal. And I sincerely hope the practice keeps my mother from forwarding any more dehumanizing garbage. However, when I confronted my father a second time in a text about his subscription to the *Epoch Times*, the right-wing

4. Matt 10:14.

135

misinformation "news" source historically rooted in anti-China and (most recently) pro-Trump propaganda, he flat-out avoided my question, that is, until they came for a visit. I was angry that he ignored me, and he knew it. To assuage my anger, my dad said he felt he would be able to spot the propaganda, and besides, he really enjoys the culture and arts section. I was disappointed by his response, and he felt that too because he said as much: *I am sorry I disappoint you.* Yes, I am so gravely disappointed, but mostly just profoundly sad.

Have my parents made a concerted effort to explore a different Christian response to the LGBTQ+ community—one *not* rooted in conditions and judgment? Has my mother done anything to change her view about gay marriage, or is she content to remain in that place? She is thoughtful, but has she shown genuine concern for this marginalized group of God's beloved children by branching out and researching new scholarly biblical commentary on the subject? My family of origin can do the necessary work to explore their own racism and prejudices—each of us chooses what we put in our basket to nurture and carry away with us.

Forgiveness also does not require or entail reconciliation—a reality that goes against every Christian teaching ingrained within me. Instead, my family's past training and child-rearing told me that if reconciliation does not occur in my relationship and friendship circles, then I should have been the one to work more diligently toward it. But one thing is for sure, you never walk away—to "give up" suggests failure and defeat. But for now, this is what makes my forgiveness so hard: I have to live with everything my family has said (or not said at all)—an incredibly painful offense—while simultaneously removing the grip this vice has over me.

Perhaps there's something to be said when Jesus says in Luke 14:26 that a true disciple must "hate his own father and mother." Just like the builder who didn't count the cost of what it would take to complete the house (Luke 14:28–30), there is a cost that we must take into consideration when we claim to be a Christ-follower. We are bound by seeking Truth and speaking Truth—as Christians, we do not have the authority to move the moral goalpost. Instead, we are bound to follow in Christ's example to put down our sword (both figuratively and literally) and to simply love. Jesus, in fact, commanded it. By so doing, it is only then that we are truly free—we no longer need to use up our energy searching for reasons to place condemnation on people whom Jesus himself did not condemn. And if I am a true disciple, I must surrender spewing hate toward another child of God through my own words, in my actions, *and with my vote.* The all-loving Jesus, who is the author of compassion, is the one I chose to follow. The cross I carry does not reflect the same Christian understanding as my family of origin, and it may just cost me the loss of those relationships.

I don't know how all of this is going to end. But I can guarantee if there is going to be reconciliation, the healing will take time. South Africa did not resolve apartheid overnight. But the folks behind the Truth and Reconciliation Commission of 1995 knew that for unification to take place, the stories of human atrocities against their fellow citizens had to be told in the public forum—there can be no unity without accountability. I believe the same philosophy of seeking accountability is true for any type of broken relationship, really. For my own healing, I thought I needed a few things. I wanted my family to take ownership of the fact that their vote for Trump contributed to and enabled the increased divide in our country. No excuses, no matter how good their intentions. Because when they can own it, they are more invested in fixing it. In addition, I needed them to go back to every one of their Republican circles and tell them about their change of heart *and why.* Encourage those people to do the same. Make a daisy chain. But that's only half of my healing. True reconciliation requires a response from each member of my family of origin, and when that doesn't come, at least not now, the relationship remains broken, *even if I have already forgiven them.*

> Growing apart doesn't change the fact that for a long time we grew side by side; our roots will always be tangled. I'm glad for that.
>
> —Ally Condie (via @melrobbins)

Bibliography

American Immigration Council. "An Overview of U.S. Refugee Law and Policy." September 20, 2021. https://www.americanimmigrationcouncil.org/research/overview-us-refugee-law-and-policy.

American Thinker. "About Us." https://www.americanthinker.com/static/about_us.html.

Benen, Steve. "Why McConnell Struggled with Questions about His 'Moral Red Line.'" MSNBC, April 8, 2022. https://www.msnbc.com/rachel-maddow-show/maddowblog/mcconnell-struggled-questions-moral-red-line-rcna23564.

Bittker, Bobby M. "LGBTQ-Inclusive Curriculum as a Path to Better Public Health." American Bar Association. https://www.americanbar.org/groups/crsj/publications/human_rights_magazine_home/intersection-of-lgbtq-rights-and-religious-freedom/lgbtq-inclusive-curriculum-as-a-path-to-better-public-health/.

Blackwelder, Carson. "Dixie Chicks Talk Cancel Culture 17 Years after Being Blacklisted." Good Morning America. https://www.goodmorningamerica.com/culture/story/dixie-chicks-talk-cancel-culture-17-years-blacklisted-69617700.

Book of Common Prayer and Administration of the Sacraments and Other Rites and Ceremonies of the Church: Together with the Psalter or Psalms of David According to the Use of the Episcopal Church. New York: Seabury, 1977.

Brennan Center for Justice. "Voting Laws Roundup: December 2021." December 21, 2021. https://www.brennancenter.org/our-work/research-reports/voting-laws-roundup-december-2021.

Brewster, Jack. "Who's More Loyal? Cheney Voted with Trump More Than Possible Replacement Stefanik." *Forbes*, May 6, 2021. https://www.forbes.com/sites/jackbrewster/2021/05/06/whos-more-loyal-cheney-voted-more-with-trump-than-possible-successor-stefanik/?sh=5422dac532e1.

Brown, Brené. "Brené on Words, Actions, Dehumanization, and Accountability." *Unlocking Us* podcast, January 13, 2021. https://brenebrown.com/podcast/brene-on-words-actions-dehumanization-and-accountability/.

Bump, Philip. "Fox News Talks about 'Cancel Culture' and Political Correctness a Lot More Than Its Competitors." *Washington Post*, January 14, 2020. https://www.washingtonpost.com/politics/2020/01/14/fox-news-talks-about-cancel-culture-political-correctness-lot-more-than-its-competitors/.

Bush, George W. "Statement by the President in His Address to the Nation." https://georgewbush-whitehouse.archives.gov/news/releases/2001/09/20010911-16.html.

Center for Faith, Sexuality & Gender. "Statement of Faith." https://www.centerforfaith.com/about/statement-of-faith.

———. "What We Do." https://www.centerforfaith.com/what-we-do.

Cohen, Rebecca, and Joshua Zitser, "A Gay Man's Mass Email to His Family Demanding They Stop Voting for Republicans Went Viral. His Dad Said It Helped Change His Mind." *Business Insider*, March 16, 2023. https://www.insider.com/viral-email-family-stop-voting-republican-changed-dads-mind-2023-3.

Corrigan, John. "Why Do White Christians in America Think They Are Persecuted?" *Canopy Forum*, June 23, 2020. https://canopyforum.org/2020/06/23/why-do-white-christians-in-america-think-they-are-persecuted/.

Crocket, Stephen A., Jr. "If Lindsey Graham Claims That Systematic Racism Doesn't Exist, Does It Make a Sound?" *The Root*, April 26, 2021. https://www.theroot.com/if-lindsey-graham-claims-that-systematic-racism-doesn-t-1846762990.

Daily Caller. "Leftist Agenda in Class: Student Dismantles Critical Race Theory in School Board Meeting." Facebook video, posted July 31, 2021. https://fb.watch/nx52DT4PDp/.

Dimock Camp Meeting Ground. Home page. http://www.dimockcampmeeting.org/index.html.

Elder, Larry (@larryeldershow). Instagram video, August 6, 2021. https://www.instagram.com/reel/CSO--35nlNw/.

Epatko, Larisa. "How the World Is Reacting to Trump's Use of S***hole." PBS News Hour, January 12, 2018. https://www.pbs.org/newshour/world/how-the-world-is-reacting-to-trumps-use-of-shole.

Evans, Rachel Held. "Inside Mark Driscoll's Disturbed Mind." Rachel Held Evans's blog, July 29, 2014. https://rachelheldevans.com/blog/driscoll-troubled-mind-william-wallace.

Farivar, Masood. "US Hate Crimes Rise." VOA News, August 23, 2022. https://www.voanews.com/a/us-hate-crimes-rise-during-first-half-of-2022-/6713791.html.

Gebel, Meira. "Baby Boomers Share Nearly 7 Times as Many 'Fake News' Articles on Facebook as Adults under 30, Study Finds." *Business Insider*, January 13, 2019. https://www.businessinsider.com/baby-boomers-more-likely-to-share-fake-news-on-facebook-study-2019-1.

Gibson, Mel, dir. *Braveheart*. Hollywood, CA: Paramount Pictures, 1995.

Giegerich, Steve. "The Right to Not Remain Silent." Teacher's College, Columbia University. March 3, 2021. https://www.tc.columbia.edu/articles/2021/march/derald-wing-sue-offers-strategies-to-disarm-and-dismantle-racism-and-bias/.

Greenspan, Rachel E. "How 'Cancel Culture Quickly Became One of the Buzziest and Most Controversial Ideas on the Internet." *Business Insider*, August 6, 2020. https://www.businessinsider.com/cancel-culture-meaning-history-origin-phrase-used-negatively-2020-7.

Gupta, Sujata. "Redefining 'Flesh-Colored' Bandages Makes Medicine More Inclusive." *Science News*, February 24, 2021. https://www.sciencenews.org/article/redefining-flesh-colored-bandages-makes-medicine-more-inclusive.

Gutiérrez, Daniel G. P. "How Will Your Vote Reflect Jesus?" The Episcopal Diocese of Pennsylvania. October 29, 2020. https://www.diopa.org/news/how-will-your-vote-reflect-jesus-10-29-20.

Heritage Foundation. "A Sampling of Recent Election Fraud Cases from across the United States." The Heritage Foundation. https://www.heritage.org/voterfraud.

Irving, Debby. *Waking Up White, and Finding Myself in the Story of Race.* Cambridge, MA: Elephant Room, 2014.

Jones, Kimberly. "How Can We Win? Kimberly Jones Powerful Speech Video Full Length Black Lives Matter #BLM 2020." CARJAM TV Chancel. YouTube video, June 9, 2020. https://youtu.be/llci8MVh8J4.

Katz, Leah (@DrLeahKatz). "WITHDRAWING is not the same thing as SETTING A BOUNDARY. It's not okay to withdraw by withholding love, speech, cordiality, because you're feeling upset/angry with someone." Instagram. May 5, 2023. https://www.instagram.com/p/Cr32qcsv3Te/?img_index=1.

Keith, Morgan. "California Recall Candidate Larry Elder Says It Could Be Argued That Slave Owners Were Owed Reparations after the Civil War." *Business Insider*, September 4, 2021. https://www.businessinsider.com/larry-elder-argued-that-slave-owners-were-owed-reparations-2021-9.

Kirk, Michael, dir. *Trump's American Carnage.* PBS Frontline. January 26 and February 1, 2022. https://www.pbs.org/wgbh/frontline/documentary/trumps-american-carnage/.

Lang, Alexander. "Christian Nationalism: How Evangelical Christianity Became a Political Religion." *Baptist News*, September 13, 2023. https://baptistnews.com/article/christian-nationalism-how-evangelical-christianity-became-a-political-religion/.

Lee, Bruce Y. "Trump Says with 'a Herd Mentality' Covid-19 Coronavirus Will Go Away." *Forbes*, September 16, 2020. https://www.forbes.com/sites/brucelee/2020/09/16/trump-says-with-a-herd-mentality-covid-19-coronavirus-will-go-away/?sh=6fe3e71dde40.

Loucaides, Darren, and Alessio Perrone. "The Media Giant You've Never Heard of, and Why You Should Pay Attention." *Open Democracy*, March 10, 2022. https://www.opendemocracy.net/en/epoch-times-media-giant-youve-never-heard-of-and-why-you-should-pay-attention/.

McCaulley, Esau (@esaumccaulley). "That was the meaning as long as I could remember. The term was gentrified, colonized, and turned toxic by people who never loved our community. That was a sin and we deserve an apology." Instagram. June 13, 2021. https://www.instagram.com/p/CQFRiUHh6l1/?hl=en.

Mikkelson, Barbara. "Clinton Body Bags." *Snopes.* January 24, 2001. https://www.snopes.com/fact-check/clinton-body-bags/.

Miller, Paul D. "Convict Trump: The Constitution Is More Important Than Abortion." *Christian Post*, December 22, 2019. https://www.christianpost.com/voice/convict-trump-the-constitution-is-more-important-than-abortion.html?fbclid=IwAR0qG6B_dfKEvcaFl45-OZdjWxkoixplrIo9HEjRlOmr8jXADIaRwNhb1-0.

@MotherWise. "To My Friends Who Are Sick of Politics." *MotherWise* (blog), posted August 15, 2017. https://motherwiselife.org/to-my-friends-who-are-sick-of-politics/.

Nigatu, Heben. "21 Racial Microaggressions You Hear on a Daily Basis." BuzzFeed, December 9, 2013. https://www.buzzfeed.com/hnigatu/racial-microagressions-you-hear-on-a-daily-basis.

Noah, Trevor. "George Floyd, Minneapolis Protests, Ahmaud Arbery & Amy Cooper." The Daily Social Distancing Show. YouTube video, May 29, 2020. https://www.youtube.com/watch?v=v4amCfVbA_c.

Nye, Kevin (@kevinmnye1). "In the gospels, Jesus is asked 187 questions. He answers (maybe) 8 of them. He himself asks 307. Maybe faith isn't about certainty, but learning to ask—and sit in the complexity of—good questions." Twitter, June 19, 2022. https://twitter.com/kevinmnye1/status/1538578040917086208?lang=en.

Obama, Michelle. "Transcript: Michelle Obama's DNC speech." CNN. August 17, 2002. https://www.cnn.com/2020/08/17/politics/michelle-obama-speech-transcript/index.html.

Pavlovitz, John. "Good People Don't Defend a Bad Man." *John Pavlovitz: Stuff That Needs to Be Said* (blog), January 12, 2018. https://johnpavlovitz.com/2018/01/12/good-people-dont-defend-bad-man/.

Price, Jared. "If you are a Christian, and can't hear #BlackLivesMatter without feeling the need to respond with a criticism that 'All Lives Matter,' then crack open your Bible and hit up Luke 15." Facebook, May 31, 2020. https://www.facebook.com/jared.price/posts/10157534760253121.

@progressivechristianity. "Just because you are right, does not mean, I am wrong. But one of those people is wrong, someone painted a six or a nine, they need to back up and orient themselves, see if there are any other numbers to align with." Instagram, April 24, 2023. https://www.instagram.com/p/Cra-UmMtksu/?hl=en.

Race Equity and Inclusion Action Guide: Embracing Equity. Baltimore: Annie E. Casey Foundation, 2014.

Smith, Erika D. "Column: Larry Elder Is the Black Face of White Supremacy. You've Been Warned." *Los Angeles Times*, August 20, 2021. https://www.latimes.com/california/story/2021-08-20/recall-candidate-larry-elder-is-a-threat-to-black-californians.

Stansbury, James. "Biden Sets His Sights on K–12 Education." *American Thinker*, July 6, 2022. https://www.americanthinker.com/articles/2022/07/biden_sets_his_sights_on_k12_education.html.

Stewart, Dante (Stew) (@stewartdantec). "Let's be clear: the word 'woke' is just another word for Black. When people are talking about 'wokeness,' they are talking about Black equality, Black dignity, and Black liberation. That is what they hate. They are anti-Black. It has always been about white supremacy and power." Instagram, January 20, 2023. https://www.instagram.com/p/Cno8jDmLku9/?img_index=1.

@thesubversivelens. "While truth does not always rest with the majority—neither does it reflexively reside with the outliers, the exceptions, the anomalies." Instagram, July 31, 2020. https://www.instagram.com/p/CDUcejjAim5/?hl=en.

Tisby, Jemar (@JemarTisby). "Someone who is not Christian described their general experience with white evangelicals as 'People who don't have any questions.' I immediately knew what they meant." Instagram, September 14, 2022. https://www.instagram.com/p/CifTlGIrmex/.

U.S. Department of Education. "U.S. Department of Education Creates National Parents and Families Engagement Council to Help Ensure Recovery Efforts Meet Students' Needs." June 14, 2022. https://www.ed.gov/news/press-releases/us-department-education-creates-national-parents-and-families-engagement-council-help-ensure-recovery-efforts-meet-students%E2%80%99-needs.

Vocal Rush. "All Good People." (Delta Rae Cover / Shelter in Place Edition). OSAVocalRush channel. YouTube, July 2, 2020. https://www.youtube.com/watch?v=VhyX8e5zBuQ.

Vogles, Emily A., et al. "Americans and 'Cancel Culture': Where Some See Calls for Accountability, Others See Censorship, Punishment." Pew Research Center. May 19, 2021. https://www.pewresearch.org/internet/2021/05/19/americans-and-cancel-culture-where-some-see-calls-for-accountability-others-see-censorship-punishment/.

The White House. "Remarks by President Biden on the Continue Battle for the Soul of the Nation." September 1, 2022. https://www.whitehouse.gov/briefing-room/speeches-remarks/2022/09/01/remarks-by-president-bidenon-the-continued-battle-for-the-soul-of-the-nation/.

Wilson, Jason. "White Nationalist Hate Groups." The Guardian, March 18, 2020. https://www.theguardian.com/world/2020/mar/18/white-nationalist-hate-groups-southern-poverty-law-center.

Zhou, Stephen. "What Psychology Offers Christians amid Political Polarization." Christianity Today, June 24, 2019. https://www.christianitytoday.com/ct/2019/june-web-only/psychology-offers-christians-amid-political-polarization.html.

Made in the USA
Columbia, SC
18 July 2024

38822941R00098